Days before Dibley

Days before Dibley

Jill Swallow

Authentic

MILTON KEYNES ● COLORADO SPRINGS ● HYDERABAD

First published 2007 by Authentic Media
9 Holdom Avenue, Bletchley, Milton Keynes, MK1 1QR, UK
1820 Jet Stream Drive, Colorado Springs, CO 80921, USA
OM Authentic Media, Medchal Road, Jeedimetla Village,
Secunderabad 500 055, A.P., India
www.authenticmedia.co.uk
Authentic Media is a division of IBS-STL U.K., a company limited
by guarantee, with its registered office at Kingstown Broadway,
Carlisle, Cumbria CA3 0HA. Registered in England & Wales
No.1216232. Registered charity 270162

British Library Cataloguing in Publication Data

A catalogue record for this book is available from the
British Library.

ISBN 978-1-85078-724-2

Cover Design by David Smart
Print Management by Adare Carwin
Printed in Great Britain by J.H. Haynes & Co., Sparkford

Contents

Acknowledgements

I wish to thank my fellow parishioners, friends and colleagues in the parishes in which I have served over the years.

Acknowledgements

I wish to thank my friend and colleague...

This book is dedicated to my husband without whom none of this would have been possible, and also to the memory of Mary Chapman, a very dear friend and colleague.

Foreword

Women are now so much a part of the Church of England's ordained ministry as priests that it is difficult to remember the days not long ago when all our clergy were male. Jill Swallow's book takes us back to that time. Drawing on her personal experiences, she illustrates some of the uncertainties and confusions with which many women in her position had to cope. That she does so with delightful touches of humour is one of the attractions of this engaging book.

At a time when the debate over women bishops is becoming more intense, it is pertinent to be reminded of the frustrations and challenges faced by pioneers like Jill who had to tread a difficult path to become priests. But, as these pages indicate, when disappointments are mixed with a sense of humour, this blend contains within itself an element of freedom.

The honesty of this account witnesses both to the real sense of vision and determination under God that was needed to bring about change; and to the importance of the art of not losing sight of the funny side of life.

It is often said that television's *Vicar of Dibley*, precisely because of its gentle and affectionate humour, has significantly encouraged the acceptance of women as Anglican priests. Now that the Church of England is in another phase of big reports and great debates, it is good to have Jill's very readable reflections – to remind us that, as the Incarnation showed, the most effective way of communicating is through human touch.

Nigel McCulloch
Bishop of Manchester

1

Who am I?

'Sit yer down, I won't be a minute.'

I did as I was told. Mr Oldfield was eighty-four, very frail and very deaf. He lived in upstairs sheltered accommodation in the large market town of Deignton. This was our first meeting. I had already spent ten minutes on his doorstep shouting through the intercom system trying to explain who I was.

'I'm the deaconess from St Philip's Church, Mr Oldfield. Mr Lockwood, the vicar has asked me to bring you your Holy Communion.'

'Yer what? Who did you say you were?'

I told him again, as clearly and as loudly as I could. The door opened, and I was invited into a dark living room. It was a hot day. The gas fire was on, the windows closed, and the television blaring out at full volume. Mr Oldfield was too frail to come to church any more. He had asked Donald, the vicar of the parish, if he could have Holy Communion at home. Donald had asked his new deaconess (that was me) to bring it, so here I was.

Whilst Mr Oldfield was out of the room, I unpacked my black Communion case that contained the bread and the wine, which had already been blessed. As reverently as I could, I set out the cross, two candles and the bread and the wine on Mr Oldfield's coffee table, and took out two service sheets from my bag. I sat back on the settee and waited. I looked round the room and waited. I looked out of the window and waited. I looked at my watch and waited.

There was no sight or sound of Mr Oldfield, so I went to the living room door and called out, 'Mr Oldfield, is everything all right?'

A voice replied from the bedroom.

'Aye – I won't be long. I'm nearly ready.'

I sat down again and waited. A few moments later, the living room door opened. In walked Mr Oldfield… without a stitch on. He was completely naked. I didn't know where to look. But he did. He walked straight across to where I was sitting, took a towel from the back of the chair next to me, and put it around his waist. Then, casting me a cursory glance he said, 'Well, come on, then.'

By this time I was on my feet. I'd never seen a nude pensioner before. I didn't know what to do. I managed to splutter back at him as loudly as I could, 'Mr Oldfield, I don't think you should be wandering round like that. Go and put your clothes back on please.'

He gave me the sort of look that suggested that I was one sandwich short of a picnic, and shouted back at me, 'What for? You're t'district nurse, aren't you? I thought you'd come to give me a bath.'

The next day, at our weekly staff meeting, I recounted the tale of my nude home Communion visit. Donald, my vicar, and, Stephen the curate, who was also a priest and another of my colleagues, fell about laughing, as of course did I. I was glad that I could laugh at myself. In 1984 deaconesses were a rare breed. Nobody knew what to make of us. I became good at laughing at myself – I think I was too good at it at times. Laughing at myself became a sort of coping mechanism. It covered much of the frustration and confusion I often felt in my new role in the professional ministry in the Church of England.

Just imagine being a GP, and there you are, in your surgery with a patient, or a teacher standing in front of your class. You are trying to act in a professional manner, and each time you try someone pipes up with the words 'What did you say you were?' And when you tell them for the umpteenth time, their only response is 'What's one of those?'

Such questions over and over again only served to undermine my professionalism and confidence as a deaconess. However, those same questions also underlined the problem. As a deaconess, my role was not recognised or understood by people in the parish.

The Church of England had already begun to select and train its male and female candidates alongside each other. At the end of the three year ordination course, only the men were ordained deacon, and usually became curates in parishes. After a further year, most male curates were then ordained priest, but still remained as curates for two more years. The women who trained alongside the men were made deaconesses at the end of the same ordination course. At that time deaconesses remained deaconesses – no ordination for us.

And just to confound confusion, a deaconess was not the equivalent of a male deacon. As a deaconess, I was one of a professional order of lay women in the Church, whereas a deacon was part of the three-fold order of ordained ministry of bishop, priest and deacon.

And so no wonder confusion, frustration and misunderstandings abounded, not just among the parishioners, but also among the Church hierarchy. This was partly why I had to resort to buying sexy purple underwear in Lent, but first I must tell you about Donald.

Donald Lockwood, my vicar, was a kind but strict and steely sort of man. He was exact, precise, prompt and tidy and did not suffer fools of any variety. Carelessness, untidiness and lateness in worship were simply not tolerated. I watched him leading worship, fully robed and from lectern to pulpit to altar, his movements were effortless and smooth. I did sometimes wonder if he was on castors. My ambition was to one day be able to glide through a service like Donald.

However, it just so happened that the archdeacon also lived in our parish, and he sometimes worshipped at St Philip's, our parish church in Deignton. Now Archdeacon John was one step down from the bishop, and therefore superior to Donald. The archdeacon was a tall, kindly, jovial, more relaxed person than Donald, and seemed to keep a bemused professional eye on how Donald was treating me, this new breed of woman, in the parish. One Sunday after the service, the archdeacon approached me at the back of church.

'Jill, I really do think that you should wear a deacon's stole when you are assisting at the altar. After all, you are acting as a deacon.'

A deacon's stole was a long, coloured scarf usually worn over a long white robe called a cassock alb. The stole was tied at the side – a bit like Miss World's sash.

When I mentioned the archdeacon's suggestion to Donald, Donald went at once into his steely determined mode: 'You may indeed act as a deacon, Jill, but the Church has not as yet ordained you as a deacon. To wear a deacon's stole is therefore inappropriate.'

No surprises there. At least I knew exactly where I stood . . . well, I did until the evening when the archdeacon was celebrating Holy Communion at St Philip's and he asked me to assist him at the altar. There I was in the vestry beforehand wearing my long blue deaconesses' cassock, when he insisted: 'Jill, you must wear a deacon's stole when you serve at the altar with me.'

This I duly did. I could hardly refuse the archdeacon. But Donald was not happy about this, and told me so in no uncertain terms the next day. This put me in a very difficult position, so I suggested, 'Donald, perhaps you and the archdeacon could discuss this together, and come to some decision and let me know, because it seems that whether I wear a stole or whether I don't, I seem to be at cross purposes with somebody.'

The weeks passed, and I sensed that Donald seemed somewhat reluctant to do this. So on the basis that I saw more of Donald than the archdeacon, I made a unilateral decision not to wear a deacon's stole again.

But then Lent came round. Lent, the name for the weeks which lead up to Easter in the Church, is traditionally a time to take stock, to look back and to look forward, and to reflect on what our faith in Jesus means to us. I soon discovered that in Deignton, Lent seemed to have been hijacked by people who went into overdrive with misery. Happy people became solemn. Seemingly carefree people became serious and studious.

Stephen, my lovely priestly colleague, had taken the 'You must be miserable in Lent' pill too – much to my surprise and dismay! There we both were on Tuesday after morning prayers, laughing and sharing experiences and anecdotes as usual. The following day, Ash Wednesday, the first day of Lent, I couldn't get a word out of him. In fact he was falling to his knees so much in the service that at one point when he genuflected right in front of me, I nearly fell over him. He and Donald were celebrating so many services of Holy Communion, in so many different places at so many times in the day, I simply couldn't keep up with them all.

The women in the church seemed to be busy doing one of two things. They were either hosting or organising evening Lent groups, or trying to outdo each other in the home-made soup and perfect sandwich department. These items were and are essential fare for any Lenten lunch group. Everybody seemed to be busy and religious all of a sudden – especially on a Wednesday night in Deignton. Just when I thought church life couldn't get much duller, it did. Donald announced to the congregation at the Sunday services: 'As is our custom here at St Philip's, beginning on Ash Wednesday and on subsequent Wednesdays in Lent, there will be a full choral evensong here at seven thirty. In place of a sermon I shall be delivering my weekly Lenten address. Those of us in this church who take our faith seriously will, of course, make this service a priority.'

So there I was in St Philip's vestry on Ash Wednesday for the vicar's Lenten address. The vestry was full. The choir had robed upstairs in their vestry, and were now arrayed on the steps. There were almost thirty people in total, and looking around I saw that every single one of them was wearing something purple. Purple is the Church's special colour for Lent. Most clergy love dressing up and Donald was no exception. He was gliding around and surveying the scene in his purple stole and chasuble. Stephen was sporting his purple stole, and he had on purple frilled cuffs, which I hadn't seen before. The altar servers each had a purple girdle round their waists. The choir was not to be outdone. Each was wearing a cross with a purple ribbon round their neck. And here I was, wearing my navy blue deaconess' cassock with my deaconess' cross. In comparison to my friends and colleagues, I was 'plain Jane' the 'poor relation'. Thanks to Donald not allowing me to wear a deacon's stole, I was the only one among all these people who had nothing purple to wear.

As we lined up to process into church, Donald delighted in inspecting his troops. His eyes eventually alighted on me.

'Looking rather underdressed, Jill, I fear,' he remarked.

Everyone smiled pityingly at me, and I smiled back at Donald and them, through gritted Lenten teeth, thinking, 'And whose fault's that?'

The answer to all my Lenten frustration revealed itself to me the following Wednesday teatime whilst I was collecting our three children, Tom, Rachel, and Julie, from school. The twins were five and Julie was four, and we were waiting for the bus from town to home. It was then that I saw it . . . right there in front of my eyes. In Balliford's department store window was the answer to any deaconess' Lenten frustrations. On a model in the window was the most exquisite set of purple satin underwear. From shoulder strap to stocking tip it really was 'the works'. I stared at it, thinking, 'Well, that will certainly liven up Lent . . . both at home and at church. And as for all the purple people in the vestry on a Wednesday night, if I can't join them, then I'll beat them. What I'm not allowed to wear on top, I'll just have to wear underneath.'

Within minutes, I'd trailed all three children inside Balliford's, and was exchanging my family allowance for a boxed set of sexy, purple satin underwear. I was now looking forward to the vicar's Lenten address with added relish and anticipation. Come six o'clock, I was 'robing up' in the bedroom. My husband Keith put his head round the door and his mouth dropped open.

'Where are you going dressed like that?'

'The vicar's Lenten address – that's where. These are my new undercover vestments.'

So complete with deaconess' cassock and undercover vestments, once more I was in the vestry and Donald was inspecting his troops yet again. His pitying eyes alighted on me once more and he shook his head.

'Still looking rather underdressed, Jill, I fear.'

This time I was able to look up and smile back confidently at him, thinking, 'Little do you know, vicar. How very true your words are.'

Now, I would be the first one to admit that stockings and suspenders are not designed for narrow, hard pews in freezing cold churches in February, but these garments were worth every penny of my family allowance because they helped me to do something very important. They helped me to deal with my frustration in a positive way. Frustration, if left to fester, can often embitter a person. This underwear taught me a valuable lesson. Ever since, I have always tried to find positive ways of coping with any frustration, setbacks and obstacles.

Donald asked me to choose a hymn for his final address, so I chose the hymn 'Come down, O Love Divine'. I chose this because of the line that talks of holy charity being my outward vesture, and lowliness becoming my inner clothing. As I stood there singing it, I thought, 'There's nothing very "lowly" about what I'm wearing.'

But then I thought that in a strange sense there was. As I looked round at all the purple people on display, I saw that lowliness was not something to be paraded around on top in front of people. Lowliness is rather like underwear. It gives support but is hidden away and covered up. Each of us knows it's there, but we can forget that it's there, and it's not for all to see. Lowliness is exactly like that.

Deaconesses were rarely given the opportunity to move within the higher circles of parish life. However, every few weeks my turn came round to assist one of the clergy in taking evensong at Mayerval Hall. This was a stately home within our parish. Lord and Lady Mayerval had their own private chapel in the grounds of Mayerval Hall, and every month the clergy of neighbouring parishes were invited to conduct evensong there. Some of the clergy and their wives simply dripped subservience and courtesy by the bucket load to Lord and Lady Mayerval, before, during and after the service. It was a delight to see. I was on duty with 'Caiaphas', and he and I were on duty only because Donald was on holiday. It was Rosemary, Donald's wife, who thought up the nickname Caiaphas for Stephen, the curate. Stephen seemed to quite enjoy it. Stephen was very 'high church' and he liked people to address him as 'Father Stephen.' He always walked round the parish in his black cassock, and liked to call the service of Holy Communion 'Mass'. Caiaphas was the name of a high priest in the New Testament, hence the name.

I walked up the long, tree-lined driveway of Mayerval Hall at six o'clock, and there was Stephen waiting for me, dressed all in black. With hands clasped, he was looking even more earnest and devout than usual. We had arranged that I should preach and lead the whole of the service. However, Donald had decreed that Stephen should be there as a priest, to pronounce the absolution and the final blessing. The absolution is the prayer in which God's forgiveness is pronounced. In both these prayers only a priest is allowed to address the congregation as 'You.' If I were on my own leading evensong, which I was from time to time, I would have had to say, 'May the Lord bless *us*' and 'May the Lord forgive *us*.' That may well be all right for some congregations, but not when Lord and Lady Mayerval were present!

Lord and Lady Mayerval were sitting on the front pew. They were right in front of my nose as I stood in the pulpit. About twenty-five people made up the congregation. By this time I had greeted Lord and Lady Mayerval, escorted them to their seats, and sung the office of evensong. I had delivered my sermon, and said the prayers. All in all we had sung five hymns, and the whole service had taken about an hour. During this time, Stephen had said two prayers and contributed about five minutes to the proceedings.

During the last verse of the last hymn, Stephen and I processed to the back and stood in the church porch, ready to shake hands and bid farewell to the congregation. Lord and Lady Mayerval were the first out of church. I soon realised that I was invisible to them both. They walked straight past me, and held outstretched hands to Stephen.

'How lovely to see you again, Father Stephen. We did enjoy the service. Thank you so much.'

Stephen did his best to remind them of my presence. 'Thank Jill. She took the service. In fact, she did all the hard work.'

Reluctantly they glanced back at me and offered me the most withering, patronising looks and uttered the words, 'Yes dear . . . well, I'm sure you're a great help to Father Stephen.' Out they went into the night.

I felt so useless and surplus to requirements. Such scenes happened over and over again. Being ignored and overlooked never seemed to get easier to live with. It was always uncomfortable. It happened in different places and with different people, but the same scenario unfolded time and time again. It appeared that only men were valued in ministry. Why was it that when God called a man, and his calling was recognised by the Church, then he was seen to have a vocation? But when God called a woman, and her calling was recognised by the Church, then she was seen by many inside and outside the Church to have just taken up a little hobby?

Stephen was very sympathetic, and I was just beginning to 'lighten up' a little as I closed the main door. The last person to leave was a small, elderly man. I shook his hand and wished him goodnight, and he wandered down the path. I was just going back into the church when he turned and came back up to me and said, 'Do you mind if I say something to you?'

'What's this?' I thought to myself. 'A comment on my sermon perhaps? If this man utters anything that even vaguely resembles a compliment, I shall throw my arms round him and kiss him.'

He sidled up to me, took me by the arm, looked me full in the face and said, 'I'll just say this and I know you won't mind . . .'

By this time I was all agog. He'd got my full attention. I offered him my patient, concerned, interested, ready-to-receive-a-compliment look.

'Do you know, love, I just want to say. . .' and he nodded towards the church, 'you look a lot younger in there than you do out here. I'll say goodnight then.'

I didn't know whether to laugh or cry. I told Stephen, and as we made our way out of the church laughing, he gave me some wonderful advice which to this day has stood me in good stead: 'As long as you let all these experiences make you better and not bitter, Jill, you'll be all right. You'll survive.'

Wise words, and on that note, complete with broad back, thick skin, and sense of humour intact, I made my way home.

2

Early beginnings

Without my two metal clips I might never have met Linda, and if it weren't for Linda, who knows whether I would ever have kept going to church?

Three years before I become a deaconess, Keith, my husband, had been transferred by the Magistrates' Courts Service up to the North-East. To us this was a strange new world of leeks, clubs and bairns. Our children Rachel, Tom and Julie were all under two. The twins could only walk to the end of the garden path, and Julie was just a few months old. I was unable to drive, and it was not physically possible for me to get on and off a bus with all three children on my own. Hence I found myself in a strange place where I knew nobody, and midweek I was housebound. Then one day, Keith, my ever-practical husband, came in from the garage and onto the kitchen table clattered two metal clips.

'See these? Well, they'll change your life. Come on . . . I'll show you what they do.'

Then, before my very eyes, my wonderful, brilliant husband had given me my passport to freedom and the outside world. With the two metal clips he fastened Tom and Rachel's double pushchair to Julie's single pram. I was free. And I was noticed. In fact it was difficult not to notice us, as we tended to take up the whole pavement when we went out. I became known as 'that woman with all those bairns.'

It was the day before Mothering Sunday and we decided to go to church the following day. I was so desperate to meet people and church seemed a good place to start. By half past nine the following morning, we had washed, changed, fed and dressed all three children and ourselves, and there we were sitting in St Martin's Church for the main Sunday service. I looked around. I could see a smattering of well-heeled elderly people and most of them were women. I soon realised, to my dismay, that we were the only family in church. There were no other children there at all. The vicar was in his late fifties, and seemed a rather jovial, pleasant man. He preached about mothers, and told us how they could enrich our lives and put God's love into action. Tom, Rachel and Julie played quite happily and quietly in the pew until Rachel decided to stretch her legs by standing on a kneeler. During the prayers, she slipped off it and banged her chin on the pew in front. Of course everyone turned round just to make us feel even worse, but her cries were soon abated by a piece of white chocolate and a cuddle. All was well.

After the service as we queued down the one aisle to shake hands with the vicar, I just ached for somebody to speak to us. A few of our fellow parishioners offered polite nods and restrained 'good mornings' but little else. The vicar was standing at the back of the church in the porch and it was now my turn to shake his hand. As I did so his jovial demeanour changed. He held out a very stiff arm towards me and a solemn face bore down on me. In front of the whole queue of people his voice boomed out, 'If your child cries again in church, take it out. We have the bishop coming next week, and I don't want *him* disturbed. Good morning.'

That was my first experience of church life in the North-East. It had been a lonely young mother who left for church that Mothering Sunday morning, and it was an even lonelier young mother who returned home.

But all was not lost. I still had my two metal clips. And with my metal clips, I got to meet Linda at the play-group. She was a single mother with two young boys, and we became good friends. I recounted my experience at church, and she laughed at me.

'St Martin's – you never went there, did you? You must be mad. You're invisible in that place, unless you're of a certain age and income bracket.'

She went on to tell me of her frosty reception there too. 'Mind you, if I'm honest, I only went there for the flowers. You see, I love flowers but I've nobody to buy me any and I can't afford any. One day, I want to get a job in a flower shop, so I thought, if I start going to church, I can learn how to arrange them. Six months I did at St Martin's.'

She made it sound like a prison sentence, and went on to tell me that every time she asked one of the ladies at church if she could be put on the flower rota, their answer was always the same.

'Not at the moment, dear. The rota's full. We will let you know if there's a vacancy.'

Evidently, one Tuesday morning Linda had had to walk through the church to get into the church hall, and she'd spotted a new lady arranging the flowers, and had gone over to compliment her on the arrangement.

'That's kind of you to say so. I knew nothing about flower arranging until a few weeks ago. In fact, I've only just moved into this parish. I must say the ladies here have made me feel very welcome.'

'That was it,' declared Linda, 'I've never been back.'

But I was determined to go back. Ever since my teens, I had felt drawn to the Church's ministry. Coming from a church family, and always having gone to church, our local bishop had once invited any teenagers in the diocese who were interested in the Church's ministry to his house one afternoon. There were about twenty boys and three girls. The three girls were the last to shake hands with the bishop afterwards, and I remember him on the doorstep making light – almost apologetically – of the few opportunities for women in the Church. Glancing across at his chaplain and then at us he had explained, 'My dears, there's nothing I'd like better than to see a young blonde female curate, believe you me, but don't forget, there's always missionary work or the possibility of becoming a nun.'

I did toy with the idea of missionary work, and I even tried my hand at becoming a nun. Being quite shy in those days, I thought I might be cut out for the convent. After spending a short time with two teaching orders of nuns, I soon decided that this was not the life for me. My reasons, I'm afraid, were very worldly. I realised only then that I wanted a family, I missed my basic home comforts (especially a mirror and a hot water bottle) and I knew that I just couldn't cope with the cold. As I'd sat with the sisters huddled round the one tiny coal fire in an upstairs turret during the daily times of recreation, I used to watch them force their chapped, gnarled and stiff hands to write and sew, and I just ached with the cold. That had been enough for me.

On leaving school, I read theology at university, and from there went on to do my teacher training. Keith and I married during the time I was teaching religious studies, and then the twins came on the scene. Even with three young children, I still had that feeling that God

had put me on one side for something. Whenever I wandered into Keith's workshop I was reminded of this feeling. Keith had always loved working with wood, and he
would never throw any piece away. 'I'm keeping it just
in case. It might come in useful . . . you never know.'
That's just how I felt that God was thinking about me
too.

So Linda and I did go back to St Martin's. Or rather I
went back and dragged Linda with me for moral support. Over the months she and I shared our frustrations
and giggles. We managed to upset the Mothers' Union
by turning up at their afternoon meetings with all five
children, and disturbing their cosy chatter. When the
vicar visited Linda and then me at home, and begged us
both to keep our children away from church on a
Sunday until they were older, we listened politely, but
decided to ignore him. Every Sunday we endured glares
and stares from the vicar's wife. Cold shoulders and
frosty looks were the order of the day for us, but we
struggled on and persevered. I don't know whether all
this strengthened our faith, or just stiffened our resolve,
but it proved to be strong glue and it bound us together.
These qualities of perseverance and good humour
turned out to be admirable coping strategies in the years
ahead.

Once upon a time at St Martin's there had been . . . Dr
Charles. Among parishioners his very name was revered
and talked about in hushed tones. Dr Charles and his
family used to attend St Martin's and Dr Charles himself
had been the local ordinand. He had been selected to
train for the priesthood. Every one of the vicar's sermons contained a reference to Dr Charles. These references included the humility Dr Charles had shown by
relinquishing his post as senior lecturer at the university
in order to become a humble parish priest. Then there

were the sacrifices Dr Charles had been prepared to make. He had had to move into more modest clergy accommodation. He had had to cope with a significant reduction in income and lifestyle. His wife had had to endure all this upheaval too, to say nothing of their children's private schooling being disrupted. The list went on and on. To the people of St Martin's, this man was a saint. Now presumably he was a reverend saint. Linda and I took bets each week on how many times Dr Charles' name would be mentioned in the vicar's sermon. There were never less than two references to Dr Charles, and sometimes as many as six.

It was against this backcloth that I tried to engage the vicar in conversation about my own sense of vocation. I outlined my background and tried to explain how for many years I had felt called to some sort of professional ministry in the Church. His answer was always the same.

'Yes, well, my dear, as you get older there'll always be the Mothers' Union, and until then you have the Sunday school, and you've plenty at home to keep you busy.'

'But I'm not just talking about St Martin's, vicar. I'm talking about ministering in the wider Church . . . professionally . . . perhaps as a deaconess.'

'No, no, no. That wouldn't be right at all. I could never sanction that. Not with all these little ones to look after. They are your priorities, my dear, and this is where you need to be – with them. Now if you'll excuse me . . .'

Try as I might, we could never get any further than that point in the conversation. Seemingly the door which had opened to allow Dr Charles to swish through by having his vocation tested and then being selected to train for ministry was very firmly closed to me, as far as my vicar was concerned. The only reason for this seemed to be that it was because I was a woman, wife and mother.

Months passed. It was Christmas, and I found myself talking about all this to a long-standing family friend of ours who just happened to be a parish priest. He offered me a lifeline.

'I've known you since you were a teenager, Jill. In all that time, you've had this sense of calling. Why don't you let me write to your director of ordinands and outline the situation to him?'

His intervention on my behalf resulted some weeks later with an appointment with the head deaconess in our diocese. Every diocese had a head deaconess, and these people tended to be elderly, single women. Our meeting together, such as it was, seemed to revolve totally around the welfare of the children, and whether my husband supported me. She told me that she would contact the bishop and inform him of our meeting, and on leaving I was handed a sheet of paper which included the following information: 'As a deaconess, you will have many calls on your time. You will not always be available for your husband and children. Meal times could well be disrupted, and there may be little time for you to cook and bake for your family as before.'

It took me all of five minutes in the car going back to decide that these considerations were not going to become obstacles for me. Serving the Church was something I'd felt a great yearning to do for many years. It was as if I needed the authority of the Church to minister to people. As a capable person, and being well organised at home, I failed to see how serving the Church as a young wife and mother would constitute child neglect in any way at all. A month later, the bishop came to visit us at home, and before long I was sent on a selection course.

It was on Good Friday 1982 that my answer fell through the letter box onto the doormat. 'You have been selected for training for stipendiary ministry as a deaconess.' I was absolutely ecstatic and danced round the room clutching my letter. Still on a high, which seemed most inappropriate for Good Friday, off we all went to church in the afternoon. The vicar seemed quite jovial too for a Good Friday, so after the service, I decided to tell him. He was standing in his usual place by the door. With a big smile on my face and eyes aglow, I shook his hand and blurted out, 'I've been accepted – accepted for training as a deaconess.'

He looked down on me, patted me on the head rather as a grandfather would a small child, and uttered the enthusiastic and encouraging words, 'Well done, dear.' He then promptly turned to the next lady behind me in the queue, and remarked on her hat. Such was life. As a mere woman I was never going to reach the dizzy revered heights of Dr Charles.

And yet, women and their families made sacrifices too. On completion of my training, I knew that the bishop would appoint me to another parish within the diocese. But unlike my male colleagues, very few deaconesses were provided with rent and rate-free clergy accommodation in parishes. In my own case, we were expected to sell our house and buy another in a much more expensive area, almost doubling an already considerable mortgage. This move was at the Church's convenience but had to be entirely at our own expense. There were no removal or resettlement grants for us. New school uniforms for the children, a much higher mortgage for us to find, and a significantly increased car journey for Keith to and from work each day – all these were a high price to pay for us too. However, what were these sacrifices compared with those of Dr Charles? We knew exactly what they were. They were costly, unrecognised, and expected.

Linda and I still took our turn at helping to run the play-
group. She was delighted at my acceptance for the
Church's ministry, and we shared many a laugh together
about the future. 'A deaconess. Just think, if you ever
have any trouble with your flower arrangers in church,
give me a call. You can bring me in as your "external flo-
ral advisor."'

I promised her that I would and asked her if I should
ask the vicar's wife to give her a reference. Linda was
still waiting to be admitted to the flower rota. The
vicar's wife ruled the ladies of the flower rota with military precision, but still Linda would not give up hope
and kept asking to join them. The last time, instead of
being informed that there wasn't a vacancy, she was told
by the vicar's wife, 'Well, you see, we like all our flower
arrangers to go on a course,' to which Linda had replied,
'Well I'll go on a course. I'd love to go on a course.'

'Yes, well, the thing is, dear, we like our ladies to have
a few months flower arranging experience here at St
Martin's, before they go on this course. I will bear you in
mind next time we're looking for somebody.'

And so it went on. The following day, we were due at
the playgroup. However on the Sunday evening, Linda
rang me up.

'I've just realised I've got to be at the dentist's for half
past ten tomorrow and I'm supposed to be on duty with
you. I've managed to find somebody to cover for me, but
if I'm a few minutes late collecting Richard and George,
can you keep them with you and your three until I get
there? I'll be as quick as I can, and I'll send them with a
sandwich each, just in case I miss the bus or something.'

By quarter to twelve the next morning, most of the
other children and helpers from playgroup had gone
home. There was no sign of Linda, so I wandered outside to the play area with my three and Linda's two and

stood watching them on the climbing frames. I heard footsteps behind me, turned round and saw a policeman.

'Could you tell me the names of all these children, please?'

As I did so, he took me to one side. 'There's been a very bad accident, I'm afraid. A Mrs Linda Hardie has been knocked down by a car a few streets away. She was on the pavement when it happened and we think the driver of the car could have had a heart attack. I'm afraid Mrs Hardie was killed instantly.'

I was numb. Like a zombie, I ushered all the children inside. The policeman asked me to stay with Richard and George until they could find a relative to come and take them home. The children were all laughing and talking as they tucked into their sandwiches. I sat watching them, but couldn't think or speak or take in what they were saying to each other. Then little George punched the air. 'Great! Traffic light biscuits. Mummy knows I like these. She makes them just for me. Look!'

He held a biscuit in front of my face and I managed to force a smile. This was the last meal they would ever eat that Linda had made for them. If only they could know how special this little packed lunch was. They might have savoured every crumb, and kept every wrapping. I would. When Linda's sister arrived, it was only then I gave way to my tears. We hugged each other for what seemed like ages. I left her alone with George and Richard, and then after a while, stunned and tearful, we all made our quiet journey home.

St Martin's was packed for Linda's funeral. The ladies of the church had done her proud. There were flowers everywhere. Linda never did make it onto their flower rota, but yet in a sense, it had taken Linda's death to bring out their finest skills. The church looked beautiful, and it was perhaps Linda's finest hour. The vicar talked about Linda's love for flowers, and how all our lives were like cut flowers, and how tragic it was when we are taken in full bloom. Since that day I have taken many funerals, and often relatives say to me before a loved one's funeral, 'We don't want flowers. They are such a waste. They just get left.'

Whenever people say this to me I always think of Linda, and how each of her funeral flowers that day was a token of love . . . and regret. Can a token of love ever be wasted? Whether it's precious ointment for Jesus or flowers for Linda, they are both marks of love and respect for an individual human life – a life that is beyond price. And love for another person is always generous and costly. By its very nature love is wasteful – and a good thing too. Which one of us would want to live in a world where love is measured out, calculated and rationed? Linda's love was spilt and spoilt. It was the generous costly sort. So to those who say, 'Flowers are a waste of money at funerals' I can only say, 'Not for Linda they weren't. They were just right.'

3

Domestic matters

I began my ordination course when Tom and Rachel had just started school. Julie was pre-school and still at home with me most days. We lived in a small house, and studying at home was an uphill challenge. Essay deadlines had to be met, and after the children were in bed, many evenings were spent with me facing the wall at my desk in the living room, and Keith wearing his earphones either listening to music or watching television. I couldn't drive and couldn't afford to learn. I had discovered that driving lessons with Keith accompanied by all three children in the back of the car begging me to stop were far from productive. Much of my time was spent waiting for buses, and walking slowly with one or all the children to and from the school, which was about a mile away from where we lived.

Time together as a family was precious although money was very scarce. A holiday for us would have been wonderful but was out of the question. Or at least it was until I read about 'The Clergy Caravan' in the diocesan magazine. This caravan was owned by a Church organisation in the diocese and was available free of charge to all clergy who, like us, couldn't afford a holiday. I rang to inquire and outlined our situation. A clergy wife with a very clipped voice had answered.

'Well, how many children did you say you have? So it's your husband who's a clergyman, is it? No? Oh you. Well, you're not clergy I'm afraid, and your husband is working, so we can't help you. Goodbye.'

Years passed without a proper holiday for us all, not just because of the lack of money but also the lack of time. Keith's holidays from work had to be taken during the fortnight of the ordination course summer school because there was no one else available to look after our children. During the time of my course I was assigned to a neighbouring parish on a pastoral placement. Parts of days were spent visiting and there were evening meetings and services to attend, as well as sermons to prepare. Keith was wonderful and ever resourceful throughout this time. After a long and demanding day in and around the courts, and after having eaten our evening meal, both he and I would bath the children and get them ready for bed, put on their coats and bundle them, and us, into the car. Regularly on cold dark Wednesday nights Keith would then drive us all on a forty-mile round trip just for me to attend a midweek lecture. He would then return home, put all the children to bed and I would come home much later on the bus... if it arrived! Summer schools, evening lectures, residential weekends, meetings, sermons, essays and pastoral work . . . this was my pattern during the ordination course, and it was all fitted in between home and the school gate by a non-driving mother, with a fantastic husband, three lovely children, and very little money. Home life was always a priority to us. Making time for friends, neighbours, birthday parties, special meals, picnics, bonfire nights and treasure hunts were every bit as important to us as all the essays, lectures and sermons.

As the ordination course drew to a close, I was sent away with all the other candidates on the pre-ordination retreat. This was a three-day retreat and we were in silence until the bishop had delivered his 'charge' on the last evening. The charge was his last minute pep talk and blessing on those about to be sent out to minister professionally in the name of Christ and his Church. Jesus delivered a charge to his disciples. However, for the bishop there were some additional matters. Twenty-six of us assembled in the chapel to receive the charge, and only three of us were women, or 'ladies' as the bishop preferred to call us. We were kept behind after the men had left, because there were particular instructions for us. We were not to wear nail polish in church, we were not to cross our legs in the sanctuary, and we were not to wear high heels in the pulpit. Susan, Margaret and I left the chapel that night with the distinct feeling that we should aim to disguise our femininity wherever possible so as not to be a distraction to others during worship. Over wine and nibbles together afterwards, we laughed about the times when we had found some male clergy leading worship to be equally distracting for us too over the years. Yet in the bishop's eyes, distraction seemed to be a one-way street. He spoke as if men were immune from it – and as if women were the cause of it.

Towards the end of my ordination course, I had received a letter from the bishop asking me to go and see Donald Lockwood, who was the vicar of Deignton, with a view to working in his parish. Just before I was due to go on my pre-ordination retreat, Donald had called round to our house unexpectedly, to bless me for my future ministry in Deignton. There were very few parishes in the diocese at the time that were willing to take a deaconess, and at least Deignton was still within fairly easy reach of Keith's work.

Deignton was a large, hilly county town of about fifteen thousand people. A road bridge, a footbridge and stepping stones all crossed the wide river, which divided the town. A large variety of shops and houses nestled in the dip, and the railway station, housing estates and schools were scattered on all the hills around.

Donald hadn't picked a good moment to call. It was mid-morning during half-term. The children were all squabbling and fighting with each other and, needing some respite from all this, I was forcing them all outside into the back garden. They didn't want to go but I was equally determined that they should. Just as I was closing the door on them, shouting 'and I don't want to hear or see anything of you for at least ten minutes,' a very refined, quiet voice at the side of me asked, 'And does that include me?'

I apologised profusely to Donald, and was just about to show him into the living room when he informed me that this was just a brief visit. He had come to give me a blessing on my future ministry, and he insisted that he could do this just as well at the kitchen table. So there we sat at opposite sides of the kitchen table. Over the toast crumbs and dishes of half-eaten cornflakes he took both my hands and proceeded to pray for me. He then stood up, leant right over the table and put both his hands on my head and blessed me. At this point I was acutely aware of three impatient heads jumping up and down at the window, shouting, 'Mummy! When can we come in? Can we have an ice-pop? Is it ten minutes yet?'

Donald seemed to be immune from these interruptions, as men often are. I was not. We concluded our time of prayer, and thanking Donald, I showed him out of the front door. As the children burst in at the back door a few minutes later, they were intrigued by Donald's actions over the kitchen table.

'What was he doing, Mummy? Why did he hold your hands? Was he washing your hair?'

Donald and his wife Rosemary had two grown-up sons. Like most clergy wives in the area, Rosemary did not work outside the home. I first met Rosemary at my interview. It was on a lovely hot summer's day, and she had answered the door wearing a pleated skirt, a short-sleeved jumper and, as my mother would say, 'sensible' shoes. She had shown me into a long, dark room lined with books. Donald was sitting at his desk, and stood to shake my hand as I went in. Some minutes later, Rosemary came back into the study with a tray of tea. I was expecting a thorough and searching interview. Perhaps I would be questioned on my stance on particular theological issues. I might have to talk about my ordination course and current reading matter, or outline my strengths and weaknesses. Donald began this probing interview by asking me, 'Now then, my dear. What does your husband think about all this work you're going to be doing?'

I'd assured him with the words: 'My husband is very supportive of all that I feel called to do. I wouldn't be here now were it not so. He has encouraged me all the way.'

'That's as maybe, dear . . . but are you going to have any more children?'

'We've certainly no intention of having any more, so I hope not.'

It had been at this point in the procedure that Donald had begun to look me up and down in a quizzical sort of way. He'd screwed up his face as if he was not quite sure how to phrase his next question. Eventually he'd found the words.

'I don't know quite how to ask you this . . . but . . . em . . . what will you wear?'

Relieved at his question, I'd replied confidently, 'Oh, in church I shall wear my navy blue deaconess' cassock with my deaconess' cross.'

'No, no dear, I don't mean in church. I know what you'll wear in church. I mean . . . er . . . well, what I mean is . . . what will you wear in the parish?'

I'd stared blankly at him. His question stumped me. I'd had no answer. As I'd glanced down at my pink blouse, black skirt and high heels, I began to feel a bit inadequate. So, somewhat feebly I'd answered, 'Well, clothes like these . . . just ordinary clothes, I suppose.'

At this, he'd winced pityingly, closed his eyes and shaken his head. Then leaning forward in his chair, he offered me a hint of the answer he was looking for. 'A retired lady missionary friend of ours always wears a very sensible navy blue crimplene suit. It never seems to date, and very smart she looks in it too.'

I'd sat there nervously rattling my teacup on its saucer. The sun had been streaming in through the window, and I'd thought to myself: 'I'm only thirty-two. I'm certainly not ready for a sensible navy blue crimplene suit yet . . . if ever! And anyway, I don't want to have to stand on people's doorsteps, at school gates, or in bus queues looking like a retired missionary. God has called me as a relatively young woman. Why should I have to try to look elderly and neutral in order to blend in with parish life? Why can't I be allowed to express that calling through the person I am?' Needless to say, I have never bought the navy blue suit . . . yet!

But during this time in the Church, when opportunities for women to minister professionally in parishes were so limited, and also in a time before the availability of affordable childcare, perhaps these were understandable questions for an elderly clergyman to ask of his new deaconess. Many deaconesses, like myself, were acutely aware of two things. Firstly, that we were pioneers. As pioneers we were preparing the way for other women to follow after us . . . perhaps into the priesthood. I and some of my colleagues didn't think that we ourselves would ever be ordained priest. Secondly, we knew that during this time we should have to exercise a good measure of patience and self-restraint. There would certainly be occasions during this time of preparation and waiting when we would have to suffer injustice in humility. Hopefully we would be able to demonstrate to some of our male colleagues and to our congregations that we were more than equal to this task.

4

Worth waiting for?

Donald was a stickler where home Communions were concerned. Midweek home Communions were for the housebound only, and woe betide any 'housebound' recipient who was spotted out of their home shopping. Donald scanned the bus queues looking for culprits as he drove round the town, and I was instructed to act as his spy for this purpose when I went to the hairdressers.

'If they can get out to get their hair done, they can get themselves down to church. You tell me if you see any of them.'

Home Communions were taken out every month, usually by Stephen and myself. Donald insisted that we wore our long, wool cassocks for every visit. This was no problem for Stephen because he always seemed to wear his cassock for everything, but it was something of a problem for me because I couldn't drive. I had a choice. I could either walk around Deignton, getting on and off buses in all winds and weathers, and then go to meet the children from school wearing my cassock, or I could robe and disrobe for each visit in every person's house. I chose the latter. Elderly communicants gave me bemused looks and seemed to quite enjoy the spectacle of me taking off my coat, kneeling down to unzip my suit bag (there was never anywhere to hang it) taking out my cassock, putting it on, buttoning it up, then realising my deaconess' cross was still underneath it, unbuttoning it, fishing out the cross, and buttoning it all up again. I then reversed this procedure before leaving.

It was whilst I was trudging up Deignton High Street one Tuesday afternoon complete with shoulder bag, home Communion case and suit bag that I spotted Stephen across the road and waved. He weaved his way through the busy traffic towards me.

'How are you getting on? Where are you off to?'

'Hang on.' I fumbled in my pocket for Donald's list. 'Twenty-seven Darley Street. A Mrs Bassett?'

I stood and watched Stephen's expression change. He grinned and then let out a silly high-pitched laugh. Passing shoppers gave us strange looks as he began to jump up and down on the spot pointing at me as if I'd done something stupid.

'Stop it. What is it? What have I said?'

He spluttered back at me, 'Oh, you'll find out. Let's have a look.' He grabbed Donald's list for closer inspection. 'Yep . . . that's the one all right. Mrs Bassett – Mrs "What good are you, then?"'

He went on to explain that whenever anybody took Mrs Bassett her Holy Communion, she always had a little job lined up that needed doing. Evidently it had all started a few years ago with a former curate, Andrew Styles.

It was Andrew who, after taking her Holy Communion one day, and being keen to make a good impression, had allowed himself to be bullied into fitting a piece of lino behind Mrs Bassett's front door. Like a fool, he managed to make quite a good job of it, and so now Mrs Bassett expected all curates to have similar DIY skills. With a broad grin Stephen continued to regale me with tales of his past visits.

'First time I went, she had me on my hands and knees underneath her kitchen sink trying to fix this leaking tap. Well, you know me . . . I couldn't do it. I tried to tell her but she wouldn't have it. She just stood there towering over me with her arms folded. As I struggled back to my feet, and after cracking my head on this kitchen sink, all she could say was, "Eeh, I don't know – call yourself a Christian? You can't even mend my tap! What good are you, then?" Same thing happened last month. There I was . . . I'd laid the table with the bread and wine, said a quiet prayer, given her an order of service, sat down in the chair opposite, made the sign of the cross, and opened my mouth to say the opening prayer when she spouts up: "Eh, before you start all that business, I've a little job wants doing first . . . I've a shelf needs putting up."'

Stephen had been ready for her this time. 'I can't put shelves up, Mrs Bassett.'

'You can't even put shelves up – well, what good are you, then?'

Still laughing we went our separate ways, and I called back at him, 'I wonder what she'll make of me?'

'Ooh, to be a fly on the wall . . . give me a ring. Let me know how you get on.'

I found my way to number twenty-seven, and rang the bell. Nothing happened, so I knocked. Still nothing happened so I shouted through the letter box. I told Mrs Bassett who I was and why I'd come. A sharp, irritable voice shouted back at me.

'Well, come in, then. No point standing out there. That bell doesn't work.'

The door was stiff, but I pushed and pushed and eventually ended up falling quite literally into Mrs

Bassett's living room. There she was in a chair, knitting. She cast me a cursory glance, and welcomed me with the words, 'He could have told you that bell doesn't work. It hasn't worked for years. Anyway, where is he . . . Father Stephen? He promised me he'd have a look at it next time he came. I don't suppose you're any good with bells, are you?'

I offered her a weak smile and shrugged my shoulders apologetically. This was a mistake. My conciliatory gesture was seen as an admission of defeat. She looked me up and down in a derisory manner, tutted and shook her head.

'No, you don't look as if you would be.'

I was determined to remain positive and cheerful in spite of this ringing endorsement of my practical abilities, so with a cheery smile I continued, 'Father Stephen and I are taking it in turns now, Mrs Bassett, to bring you your Holy Communion every month. He'll be back next month when it's his turn, but you've got me today.'

'Have I? Well, I suppose I shall just have to make do with you then, won't I.'

With this resounding note of confidence in my mind and the clicking of her knitting needles in my ears, I proceeded to set the small coffee table. Once the cloth, cross, candles, bread and wine were all in place, I carefully placed the order of service on Mrs Bassett's chair arm, and sat down opposite her by the fire. She eventually put her knitting down and looked across at me, so I began with the opening words of the service, 'The Lord be with you' to which her response was, 'Eeh . . . I don't know, I can't make head nor tail of this.'

Thinking that she might have got the order of service upside down or back to front, or not be wearing the right glasses, I went across to see if I could help. As tactfully as I could I pointed out the opening words. 'We're just starting up here, Mrs Bassett, at the top of the page.'

She wafted me away with her service sheet. 'Nay . . . I know where I am with all that. It's not that. It's this . . . this here! This here knitting pattern . . . I can't fathom it. You might as well have a look at it now you're here.'

I wilted inside my confident exterior and admitted defeat with the words, 'I'm afraid I'm not very good at knitting, Mrs Bassett.'

At this she rounded on me. 'Yer what? They send you out into folks' homes and you tell me you're not very good at knitting. Well, what good are you, then?'

Donald told me that Mrs Bassett, who was in her eighties, had attended church most of her life. She had sung the hymns, said the prayers, given her time and money, and yet, she seemed totally incapable of showing even a glimmer of appreciation or encouragement to anyone. The whole notion of being thankful for what God had done for her had completely passed her by. How could this happen after a lifetime of church attendance? It had. It did. It was very sad.

However, in those days when I had to get used to squeezing every ounce of encouragement from even the most grudging of compliments, it was amazing how often encouragement and opportunities for ministry came from the most unexpected quarters, in unlikely places, and often from outside church circles. Take Eric Todd for instance. Eric lived in one of the old people's bungalows down in the town centre. I had first met him when I took the funeral of his wife a few months earlier. Although Eric had never darkened the doors of a church in his life, whenever I called, he greeted me like a long-lost relative. It was in Eric's house one day that I had one of those 'by the way' moments. These were moments in ministry, usually at the tail-end of a long conversation with somebody, when you discovered something absolutely vital about that person's life. Moments like this might include:

'By the way, did I tell you I have a son I've never seen?'

'By the way, this is a photo of my daughter . . . she was killed you know.'

'By the way, I never tell anybody this, but I've got a brother in prison.'

Eric's 'by the way' moment was however somewhat less serious.

'By the way, I don't know whether I should be asking you this, but I think we know each other well enough by now so I will . . . are you any good at making Yorkshire puddings?'

Relieved, I smiled back at him. 'Well, I should be. I come from Yorkshire.'

'It's just that all these years I've looked after my wife, I've had to do everything for her. I'm a good cook really, although I say it myself. In fact, I can turn my hand to most things. It's just Yorkshire puddings. I can't get 'em to rise for love nor money. I don't know where I'm going wrong.'

'I tell you what, Mr Todd. I can't stop now, but you get yourself some plain flour, eggs and milk in for next Wednesday. I'll come back then and we'll have a go . . . How's that?'

He beamed back at me. 'Champion, love . . . I'll be ready.'

I skipped back up the hill with a new spring in my step. At last, here was something I could do that Stephen and Donald couldn't! This was a pastoral opportunity that few of my male colleagues would ever get . . . or even want. Whether it was making Yorkshire puddings, or washing someone's feet, I was going to make the most of it. In those days when women really only hovered on the brink of professional ministry in parishes, I was all too aware that I (and women like me) were accepted by a few of our colleagues, tolerated by others, and loathed by many within our own Church structures. Yet here was one man who had welcomed me and accepted me into his home without question and had given me an opportunity for ministry. I wandered back home thinking of all those times when some religious people, who should have known better, refused to recognise Jesus' ministry too. Time and again, Jesus found that it was the unexpected person – often some-body who everybody thought didn't matter very much – who ministered to him most effectively. Perhaps it had to be like that for some of us who were called by him to minister in his name. If so, I was in good company.

The following Wednesday, Donald, Stephen and I met for our weekly staff meeting. Whilst Donald was answer-ing the telephone, Stephen looked over my shoulder at my open diary in which I'd written: 'Y.P. – 11 a.m.'

'Young people – 11 a.m.? What's that all about?'

I muttered back at him, 'Never you mind. Anyway, it's not young people, it's Yorkshire puddings.'

As I stood on Eric Todd's doorstep later that day, a wonderful smell of roast beef wafted out towards me. I could hear voices – men's voices – coming from the kitchen. Eric came out to meet me, and as he did so he called back into the house, 'Yes, it's her . . . t'lady vicar. I told you she'd be here.'

I was taken into the kitchen and introduced to two of Eric's neighbours. Frank and Bob were widowers and both had worked for the gas board.

'They're in't same boat as me where Yorkshire pud-dings are concerned . . . so they've come to watch. You don't mind, do you? Didn't think you would. Now, have you got everything you need?'

All eyes were on me as I began my demonstration. I went through the quantities, consistency, size of tin, oven temperature, and finished by telling them, 'The fat in your tin must be hot enough to spit at you . . . like this.' I poured the batter in the tin with a flourish, put it in the oven and sat down. Eric began to make the gravy, as Frank and Bob stared through the glass oven door watching the pudding rise and change shape.

Frank turned to me.

'So you're t'lady vicar, are you?'

'No, I'm not a vicar. I'm a deaconess.'

'What's difference? Same job, in't it?'

'No, not really. A deaconess does the same training as a vicar, but because I'm a woman I can't be a vicar. There are things I'm not allowed to do. I'm not allowed to bless the bread and wine and I'm not allowed to marry people.'

Frank was aghast. 'Yer what? They've had you doing t'same training, then they won't let you do t'same job? Have you heard that, Bob?'

Bob took up the cause. 'I have that. And you say you've done t'same training as them't do. Phew! Women would have never stood for that in our place, would they? We'd have had a riot on us hands. I'll say this for you, love . . . what you do must mean a lot to you, to have to put up with that sort of treatment. Not many folk would stand for that sort of thing nowadays.'

I smiled a resigned sort of smile. 'Well, that's just how it is for now. I knew all this before I started. But you never know, it might change one day.'

'Well let's hope so,' chimed in Frank, glancing back at the oven. 'Anyway love, never mind what you can't do. Just look at that pudding . . . that's summat you can do. Look sharp with that gravy, Eric . . . t'pudding looks ready.'

Over the clatter of plates and cutlery at the kitchen table I learnt about their families, school days, and working lives in Deignton. Over the washing up they laughed about lifetimes of mistakes and missed opportunities. As I put on my coat, picked up my bag and made for the door, Bob, still with his hands in the sink, called back at me, 'Eh, we're not right good with pastry either you know. Why don't you come back sometime and we can have another do?'

I left them laughing and talking, and wandered up the hill to St Mary's primary school where I was due to take an assembly. I liked school assemblies because, along with funerals, they were responsibilities I was allowed to undertake by myself. I didn't have to have a priest standing by my side. That day I was to tell the children about the first English martyr – St Alban. For this purpose I had acquired Donald's long black priest's cloak with a hood. It drowned me from head to foot, but it seemed to impress the children. I stood at the front of the assembly hall draped in black with my hood up. The children were drawn into the story of how Alban borrowed the priest's cloak and pretended to be a priest, enabling the real priest who was hiding in his house to escape a certain death. One hundred and eighty pairs of eyes were fixed on me as I quietly and dramatically explained how Alban was then arrested and taken away by soldiers. Mouths fell open and there were gasps when I told them that Alban was then decapitated.

After the assembly, quietly pleased with my stunning performance, I made my way up the stairs to the staff room for a coffee with Hazel, the school secretary. As I was leaving the school some time later, a whole class of children in their shorts and vests was queuing down the steps waiting to go into the hall for their PE lesson. I saw a hand shoot up in front of me and I became aware of a little boy with a very pressing question.

'Deaconess Jill, Deaconess Jill – you know that St Alban? Well, did he still have his hood up when his head was chopped off?'

I stifled a smile and put his mind at rest with the words, 'I think he would have done, don't you?'

The younger children were having their playtime as I walked out into the yard, and another little boy was lying down, right in front of the school gate. As I stepped round him I said, 'What a place to lie down.'

Indignantly he looked up at me. 'I'm not lying down. I'm playing.'

'What are you playing at?'

'Good Samaritan. I'm that man who gets beaten up, and nobody helps him and then this Samaritan comes.'

'So where's *your* good Samaritan?'

He sighed. 'I think he's gone to the toilet, but he's coming back.'

It was time to collect my own children from school so I set off through the town. It was market day and shoppers were everywhere. Iris Baines was standing outside her shop doorway. Iris' shop was a treasure trove. She sold everything from mousetraps to easy chairs. She attended church most Sunday evenings but, after the service, usually bypassed me and made straight for Stephen and Donald. Now was my chance. I was determined to make her speak to me. As I pushed through the shoppers, I smiled and managed to touch her arm.

'Hello, Miss Baines, remember me? I'm the deaconess from St Philip's.' She was every bit as nonplussed as she was on a Sunday, and she stared back, straight through me.

'Oh yes, so it is. I didn't recognise you without your robes. Anyway, don't worry – you don't look any worse.'

Another day, another compliment! Who cared? It was Friday. Keith and I relished our Friday evenings at home together with the children. There were never enough evenings in together as a family and Friday nights were always closely guarded. This was the children's 'staying up' night, and woe betide us if we forgot it! After our meal we would watch television or play games, and then during the chaotic bath times and bedtime stories, I would usually end up acting the fool with the children. Then, later on in the evening, Keith and I settled down with a bottle of wine and laughed and chattered our way through the past week. It was while we were doing just that that the phone rang.

'Are you that lady from the church who visits people? Well, do you ever visit people who don't come to church? We're thinking about having a christening, but we don't know whether we're allowed.'

I assured this lady that we did visit people who didn't come to church, and I arranged to speak with her the following week. I walked back into the living room muttering, 'Honestly, is that what people think about us in the Church . . . that we only bother with those people who bother about us? Doesn't say much for Christianity, does it?'

The following week, having discussed the matter with Donald, I was dispatched to go and visit this family with a view to baptism. Mrs Ireson, the lady who had telephoned me, showed me into a tiny sitting room, where I was introduced to Mr Ireson. Their daughter Amy, who was seven, was playing on the floor. Angela, who was thirteen, was sprawled out on the settee under a quilt; Jamie, sixteen, was just about to go out. Last but not least, was the tiny, white bundle of baby Sharon who was promptly placed in my arms the minute I sat down. I never struggled for words with a baby in my arms, and we were soon deep in conversation about sleepless nights and feeding patterns, and all the other accompanying things that tiny babies seem to bring with them into the world. Through all this chatter, however, I became aware of a certain reservation amongst them all. It was as if they were not quite sure how to say something to me, and almost as if they were holding something back.

It was only when I began to ask Mr and Mrs Ireson for their full names that I found out what that something was. After my question, there were uncomfortable sideways looks to each other and eventually Mrs Ireson broke the awkward silence.

'Well, that's it, you see. I couldn't tell you on the telephone. That's why we wanted to see you really . . . because we don't know whether we're allowed to have a christening. You see, me and him . . .' (she nodded towards her husband) 'we aren't actually Sharon's parents. It's our Angela. She's Sharon's mum. She were only twelve when she had her.'

I looked across at Angela, only a child herself, curled up on the settee.

'I am sorry, Angela. I got that all wrong, didn't I? Let's start again.' She smiled across at me and assured me that it didn't matter. 'Can any of you put into words for me why you would like to have Sharon christened?'

I half expected another awkward silence at this stage, but it was as if I'd opened the floodgates. My question resulted in hugs and hankies all round the room. Eventually it was Mr Ireson who waded into this sea of stifled sobs. 'I'll tell you why. We've been through hell and back this last year. When we look at our little Sharon, we feel so guilty because none of us wanted her. Go on, you tell her, Doreen.'

Mrs Ireson continued: 'When Angela got pregnant, we just couldn't face it. She wasn't that sort of girl. We just hit the roof, her dad and me, when we found out. What with all the neighbours talking, and all her school friends gossiping about her, we thought that the best way was just to get rid of it. You thought so, didn't you, Angela? We made all the arrangements, and it was soon after that that Angela kept getting these pains in her leg. One day she just collapsed. Her leg gave way and she just collapsed on the pavement. To cut a long story short, after all sorts of tests, they found out that she had a cancer behind her left knee. We didn't know what to think. We'd been so angry with her, and now we were just frightened to death of what might happen to her. All that mattered was keeping Angela alive . . . as for the baby, we never thought that we would be lucky enough to keep both of them. We've been living on a knife-edge . . . never prayed as much in all our lives. We've prayed when we've not known what to pray for. Angela's had to lose the lower part of her leg. We've had all that to cope with, and then the birth, and now, well . . . here we are. I don't think there can be anybody more thankful to God than all of us here. He's worked a miracle for us, and no mistake. How can we not thank him? All our family back together again, and a beautiful little baby as a bonus . . . that's why we want her christened. Is it enough?'

I stared back at them all with tears in my own eyes. Anger, fear, anxiety, guilt, and now overwhelming gratitude – this little family, who didn't know whether they were allowed to have a christening, had certainly been to hell and back. As I sat with them all, my mind wandered. I remembered the woman who didn't think that she was worthy of Jesus' attention, so she pushed through the crowd and just managed to touch Jesus' garment. What did he do? He turned and gave her his full attention.

Mrs Ireson interrupted my thoughts. 'We'll never forget what he's brought us through, and every time we look at our Sharon and Angela, we'll think of him.'

I was sure they would too. We said a prayer together, and I could see the relief and joy in their faces when they realised that baby Sharon could be baptised. This little baptism group was full of gratitude, and was in such sharp contrast to so many others where the parents only concern seemed to be with the date and the time of the service. As we clutched our mugs of tea, I assured them that we would be absolutely delighted to welcome Sharon into the Church family, and that I would do everything in my power to make the service meaningful and special.

5

Left behind

I had been a deaconess for almost a year. My fellow male students, with whom I had trained and who had been ordained deacon with me the previous year, were to be ordained priest in the cathedral the following week. This was a difficult time for many deaconesses. Our ordination training and the ordination service in which we'd been made deacons and deaconesses had been a wonderfully inclusive and happy time. Now came the parting of the ways. As far as the women were concerned it was a case of 'thus far and no further.' The men were to go forward to priesthood, but the door was firmly closed to the women who would be left behind. Our humanity was the wrong shape for the Church.

'You must bear it with good grace and fortitude, for that is the way it is,' Donald informed me.

Easy words to say as long as you were not the one who had to bear it. Easy to say from the security of a comfortable vicarage where your role in the community was well known and accepted, and where your calling by God was recognised by the Church. But bear it I had to. I was surprised at the way it affected me, because I actually did enjoy being a deaconess. Although there were constraints, frustrations and challenges in this pioneering ministry, I was also discovering that there was a significant element of freedom within it. There were no preconceived notions and expectations of what a deaconess should or shouldn't do. Many of my male colleagues felt that they were hemmed in, as they often struggled to conform to centuries of parishioners' expectations of their parish clergy. I was free from that. The fact that nobody knew what to make of me was certainly frustrating, but it was also liberating. As my fellow curates were being groomed for priesthood, I was free (as free as I could be under Donald's beady eye) to improve my skills, explore possibilities in ministry within the parish, and with the help of those inside and outside the Church, to reflect and work on my strengths and weaknesses. I liked that.

However, the ordination to the priesthood of my male colleagues also underlined how incomplete a deaconess' ministry was. The choir and congregation would always see me at a priest's side in the main services of the church. I took directions from the officiating priests in the vestry, and I stood at their side and assisted them in the Sunday services. This was the way it was for all curates too, but for deaconesses it was somewhat different. For them, this would be the pattern of their ministry in the future too. There were very few, if any, posts of responsibility in parishes for women. As well as feeling pangs of inadequacy at having to justify myself whenever a parishioner inquired of me 'Are you still in training?' or 'When will you be as fully qualified as Father Stephen?' my role did seem to be serving a more subtle purpose in the parish. The whole issue of women priests sharply divided the Church, and my presence beside the altar week by week brought this issue into sharp focus for some people. This major theological issue had taken on a human face within their parish, and parishioners had to respond in some way. My presence seemed to encourage some of those who had so far shuddered at the very thought of women priests, to soften or question or embed their own fixed viewpoints.

The ordination day arrived and I was in the cathedral sitting with my fellow deaconesses. The archdeacon had been extremely sensitive and, prior to the service, had taken the trouble to visit the three of us who had been made deaconesses alongside our fellow deacons the previous year. He had also ensured that there was a prayer in the service for 'many of the women who felt the pain of exclusion at this time.' As mere spectators we each wore our deaconess' cross and looked on as all our male colleagues knelt at the altar rail. In a packed cathedral, the bishop, the archdeacons and various parish priests gathered around each candidate in turn. They placed their hands on each man's head as the bishop said, 'Send down the Holy Spirit upon your servant . . . for the office and work of a priest in your Church.'

I was now only an observer into a closed world. I was being left behind on a journey. As I watched from a distance, I saw only men passing on the Holy Spirit to men. I glanced round and saw elderly deaconesses who had served the Church faithfully for many years. Even they, with their years of experience and wisdom, ministering in Christ's name, were not thought worthy of inclusion in the process of passing on the Holy Spirit to men. How could this be right?

Keith and I travelled home in silence. There seemed so little to say. I had received lots of cards from kind people telling me that I was in their thoughts at this time, but none more touching than this one from Mavis Robinson. Mavis had a ten-year-old son who suffered from cerebral palsy. He could neither walk nor feed himself. She was a widow, and a few months earlier her daughter had discovered that she had cancer. I picked up Mavis' card from the mat and read it as I wandered back into the living room. I was so moved by her words.

> Jill, never think that when you are standing by the altar week by week, that you are useless or not needed. You are there to represent people like me, who have to live with situations in life that we can do nothing about, and just have to get on with. You show us how to do this with patience, gentleness and good humour – and you do it beautifully. Don't stop giggling for Christ's sake. Love, Mavis.

I sat down and only then did I give way to my tears – tears of profound sadness, but also of hope.

Church vestries could be strange places. They were often untidy, draughty and damp. Occasionally (depending on the priest) they were neat and well ordered, but this was unusual. Dog-eared rotas and tables of fees, long out of date, would be found affixed to flaking walls. Sometimes a carefully folded supermarket bag was on show. This would contain clean altar cloths, discreetly left by some elderly lady in the congregation. The service register was often placed in the middle of a gritty desk surrounded by half a dozen dried up pens and broken pencils. Scattered around the vestry there would be forms to fill in, agendas for future meetings, piles of service sheets from weeks gone by that no one knew what to do with, obsolete service books kept 'just in case', Christingle candles from last Christmas, and the big wooden cross that the children decorated on Good Friday still propped up in the corner.

The priests' special robes, or vestments, were always meticulously kept. They were folded in the long, flat drawers of the vestment chest. This chest was the one glimpse of perfection amidst all this cold damp chaos. On the wall of St Philip's vestry had to be the world's most boring calendar, which never failed to bring a smile to my face. This calendar had been produced by one of our local undertakers, and the picture on it was an attempt to cheer up the peeling plastered walls by reminding us all of happier times ahead. The picture on the calendar flaunted before us 'Headstone of the Month'!

For years vestries had been men-only places. I well remembered as a teenager the mystique surrounding the church vestry. Women in the choir vestry only looked on as men and boys swished in and out of this very private room in their robes, always closing the door behind them in case we lesser mortals glimpsed something we shouldn't. Some of the tutors on my ordination course had been surprised to learn that there were women candidates who didn't even know how to assist a priest at the altar when he was celebrating Holy Communion. This came as no surprise to me. Some of us had never even been allowed anywhere near the door of a priest's vestry, let alone an altar. This was strange and new territory.

Like the vestry calendar, my Thursday evenings were set in stone. From six thirty to seven thirty I was usually marooned in St Philip's vestry, for the 'vestry hour'. This was a time during the week when people came to book weddings and arrange baptisms. Some weeks there would be a queue of people to see, and other weeks hardly anybody would come at all. Our church was set in a large graveyard, well away from the main road. Every Thursday night I was very aware of being on my own in this dark, lonely place without either a car or a telephone. I hesitated to mention all this to Donald, in case I got another of his 'this is the job you've chosen to do' lectures.

One thing I had learnt so far in parish life as a deaconess was that 'paving the way' for others was as much
about knowing when to keep quiet as it was about
speaking up. For now, it was important for me to con-
centrate on becoming competent in, and positive about,
all that I was given to do, in the hope that one day I and
others might be offered the opportunity to perform
those tasks many of us longed to do. So I soon learnt the
hard way in staff meetings, within reason, to just get on
with whatever Donald asked me to do.

My first 'this is the job you've chosen to do' lecture
from Donald was just before Christmas. Whilst Donald
and Stephen were talking about how busy their wives
were in the run up to Christmas, I decided to seize my
chance. Being a wife myself and the only one on the staff
with a very young family, I inquired, 'Do you think I
really need to be present at the eight o'clock Christmas
morning service?' I didn't think that this was such an
unreasonable request, bearing in mind that my presence
was expected at all three services on Christmas morning,
and I hadn't been asked to do anything in any of them.
However, Donald saw my request as an opportunity to
deliver one of his stern lectures on the responsibilities
and sacrifices in ministry. No allowances were to be
made for me. I decided to let this pass. There would be
other more important matters where I knew that I would
have to stand firm because of longer term implications;
however, this domestic matter was not one of them.
Although it seemed harsh at the time, as Donald
informed me, 'such is the life you've chosen.' I knew I
had to just get on with it.

My ideal vestry hour would be when a couple came to
see me just before seven thirty. Then I could ask them to
stay with me whilst I switched off all the lights and

locked up. If they were very kind they would then accompany me down the long, unlit path that led out of the graveyard and onto the main road. Here, I thanked them profusely and breathed a sigh of relief. My ordeal was over for another week. Stephen and Donald sometimes arranged wedding rehearsals for Thursday nights during my vestry hour, and expected me to take them. Convenient as this may have been for them, it was not very satisfactory for me or for the couple concerned. There was a lack of pastoral continuity with this situation, and I decided to raise this at the staff meeting. As a deaconess I was not allowed to conduct weddings, and although I knew the wedding service well enough, Stephen and Donald each had their own way of doing things within the service. In addition to this I wasn't always able to answer many of the last-minute questions which couples often asked me. This was frustrating for them, and the whole situation left me feeling unprofessional. Donald listened carefully at the staff meeting. As a result he reluctantly informed me that he and Stephen would, whenever possible, conduct their own wedding rehearsals from then on. I was uneasy about the words 'whenever possible'. I reminded them that it should usually be possible, because they were the ones who made the date for the rehearsal with the couple concerned.

Their reply to this was, 'Yes, well, as you know, Jill, sometimes things crop up in parish life at a moment's notice.'

I rested my case thinking, 'Yes, and it's amazing how many things seem to crop up at a moment's notice on a Thursday night.'

However, all these minor matters were put into context for me at the hairdressers the next day. A young girl was drying my hair, and amidst the noise of the music and the dryers, she shouted at me through the mirror, 'Do you go out to work?'

'Yes, I work for the Church.'

'Oh, do you? Which one?'

'St Philip's. That one just up the road.'

'Oh, I've been in that one. My friend got married there last year. I don't think it was you who took the service though.'

'No, it wouldn't have been me. Women aren't allowed to take weddings in our church.'

Hearing this she turned off the dryer, put both hands on my shoulders and a dreamy look came across her face as she smiled at me in the mirror and said, 'Well . . . It's no wonder that, is it? I mean you can understand why, can't you? We're all the same, we women . . . always cry at weddings don't we? Well, I do, anyway. That'll be why you can't take them. I should think so anyway.'

She turned her dryer back on, and I shrugged my shoulders and smiled back at her through the mirror. I thought about all the high-powered theological debate going on about this very issue. For this young girl it was all so simple. Women cry. That's it.

6

Know your place

Private conversations were going on at the back of church between Donald and the churchwardens. I could sense that dates and times and arrangements were being discussed, and I didn't know why. I was soon to find out. Donald eventually informed me and others that St Philip's was to get another curate. His name was Tony and he was married with a small son. He was to be ordained deacon and the diocese was to provide him with a house in the parish.

I couldn't help but feel somewhat envious at this news. I knew where this house was. There were two reception rooms, a kitchen and a study. What utter luxury! Keith and I and the children really struggled in the little semi we had had to buy for ourselves. I had nowhere to study unless all the children shared one bedroom, which was far from ideal. When there was an evening meeting in our house, Keith and the children had to spend the time around the kitchen table. There was nowhere else for them to go. If someone wanted to come and talk with me privately in the evening about something, it didn't feel appropriate or professional to take that person into the kitchen. And so I did feel slightly green. It was as if Tony's ministry and professionalism was to be recognised from the outset by the parish and by the diocese in a way that mine was not. His appointment underlined this fact. The way he was prepared for and, as I was later to find out, welcomed, only served to underline his importance and my insignificance to the Church.

There was to be a special meal to which Tony and his wife Anne, Donald and Stephen and both churchwardens were to be invited. Representatives of our parish were to attend Tony's ordination. He was to be officially welcomed at the main Sunday morning service, after which there would be a buffet lunch for the whole parish. It became painfully obvious – and I became acutely aware – that a new curate's welcome to the parish was somewhat different to that of a new deaconess. My welcome in the church hall one Sunday night after evensong had been lovely, but it had been nothing like this. However, rather than let these feelings fester, I decided to bring them out into the open with Donald.

His understanding, patient face nodded slowly towards me as he listened. I tried to explain the impact that this whole situation was having on me, and finished off by saying 'I can't help but compare myself to Tony. As a curate, his calling is recognised and provided for in a way that mine is not. This just doesn't seem fair when both he and I are called by the same God.'

Donald sighed and then nodded. 'Perhaps I have been insensitive by not always including you in the process so far, and for that I am sorry, but you must understand that Tony is being prepared for priesthood. His role as a curate is defined, whereas yours is not. One day he will become a vicar of a parish, and I have to work with that knowledge. You and I have to live and work within the constraints of the Church as it is at the moment . . . as difficult, uncertain, and as frustrating as that is . . . especially for you, but also for me and others too.'

I knew he was right, but I felt better for voicing my feelings with him. It was important not to allow these frustrating circumstances to define me. In time, perhaps, these difficulties would reveal the sort of person I was, and the person God wanted me to be. The frustration I often felt in ministry was already encouraging within me qualities of resilience, patience and good humour. And, as I continued to observe all the constraints and expectations placed on this new curate before he had even arrived, I was glad that my undefined, unrecognised ministry had at least got its freedoms as well as its limitations.

Later that day, I was just putting a meal in the oven, when there was a knock at the door. My number one pensioner was on the doorstep. I first met Bill in St Philip's a few weeks before I became a deaconess. I had gone to a midweek service as an anonymous parishioner, to just get a 'feel' for the place before I started working in Deighton. Bill had been on duty and had given me a hymn book as I walked in. He struck me from the outset as a very upright, courteous, military-looking gentleman complete with walking stick and twinkle in his eye. As I'd made my way to the door after the service, he'd asked me where I lived and begun to tell me about St Philip's.

'We've two vicars here . . . both very different. That's good. We like that. There's Donald . . . he's in charge. I like him. Not everybody does, mind you, but I do. You know where you stand with him . . . bit like me. Then we have Stephen. Now he can be a bit high and mighty sometimes when he takes the services, but he's none the worse for that. He comes down to our level and he can laugh at himself, so he's all right for us. We're used to him now. He's a good man.'

At this point, Bill had looked round furtively. As he steered me towards the door, he'd brought his head down closer to mine and lowered his voice.

'Mind you, it's all going to change soon. We've just been told that we're getting one of those awful women in a few weeks' time . . . a deaconess. You know, one of those bossy women you see on the television . . . always shouting at people and waving their banners. You know what they're like!'

'Ooh, I do know what they're like. I've seen them.'

'Yes, well, you'll know then, won't you. We've no idea what she looks like. Mind you if those you see on the television are anything to go by, they all look alike . . . boring and frustrated. Anyway, we'll just have to wait and see, won't we? Somebody has to have them I suppose . . . just our luck to be us! Now, we do hope we see you back here again before too long though. Do you think you might come back?'

I'd laughed. 'Oh yes, I'll definitely be back, but probably not for a few weeks. You see, I don't quite know how to tell you this, but in a few weeks' time . . . I'll be coming back as one of those awful, bossy women. You see . . . I'm your new deaconess.'

For a few moments he'd been lost for words. He'd then looked me full in the face, put both hands on my shoulders and we'd both thrown back our heads and burst out laughing.

'Whatever must you think of me? I mean you're nothing like . . . I would never have known . . . you don't look . . . well, you know what I mean.'

'I know just what you mean and I don't mind a bit. Anyway you can rest assured, I've no banner and I don't shout very often, but I do like to laugh and I like people who make me laugh. You have, Bill. Thank you.'

Since that day, Bill had become a good personal and family friend. He often called round to talk about his wife's illness, his latest battle with the local council or his 'remedies' for the social problems of the day.

As I took his coat he asked me, 'Was it you I saw in the bus station the other day waiting for the Symmington bus? Did you have the afternoon off or something?'

'Yes, it would be me. I'm allowed half a day every other week for my post-ordination training . . . or, as we all know it, "potty" training. That's where I'd be going. I've chosen to do some work with a priest in Symmington.'

I hesitated to use the word 'chosen'. As a deaconess, I nearly wasn't allowed to choose anything. Post-ordination training was a real choice for both Stephen and Tony. Stephen had chosen to explore some of the Church's ancient hymns with one of the brothers at the local friary, and Tony, our new curate, had asked to work with one of the homeless charities as part of his training. I wanted to do some work on communication and preaching, and had spotted an opportunity to do this one evening in St Philip's during a recording of hymns for the World Service. The compère for this service was a clergyman who presented religious programmes on local radio. From the pulpit he'd 'held' the packed congregation in the palm of his hand. He'd spoken warmly and simply about profound truths, and he'd communicated in such an informal, intimate way that I'd felt as if he were talking just to me. I knew I could learn from this man. However, I was soon to learn that Donald had other plans for me.

'I've already organised your post-ordination training for you. You are to go down to Mary Sumner House in London and learn more about the work of the Mothers' Union.'

'But Donald, I've a great deal of respect for the Mothers' Union, but that's not something I want to do. Communication and preaching is my area of interest. And I think I'd like to learn more about that from Dennis Lord.'

'Dennis Lord? You'll learn nothing from him. All you'll learn from him is how to be late for services and always look a mess. The man is an absolute shambles. He has no sense of organisation whatsoever.'

'Yes, but in the pulpit, Donald, he has people hanging on his every word, and you can hear a pin drop. That's what I want to learn about . . . how to do that.'

'Well, as I say, you're not going to learn much from him, and I can't pretend that I'm happy about it, but if that's what you want to do I won't stand in your way. But remember . . . I know that man. I've worked with him.'

My afternoons with Dennis Lord were like a breath of fresh air. However, his relaxed manner in front of a microphone bore absolutely no relation to how he lived. Dennis was a shy, awkward, reticent man who lived alone in a chaotic house full of displaced furniture. There was a standard lamp in the middle of the room, a Welsh dresser halfway across the window, and books, papers and used cups everywhere. But Dennis had this marvellous ability to unpack dry, old theological truths, dust them down, give them a revamp and then package them in everyday language for others to pick up and look at. So, in and among the dust and the used coffee cups, I learnt about timing, the use of language, the importance of finding an angle, use of dialogue and most important of all, how to communicate with people rather than preach at them. Donald remained unimpressed but I felt excited and enthused by it all. I tried to communicate some of my enthusiasm to him at staff meetings, but my contribution was always received with a polite silence and a stony glare, followed by his standard reply.

'Hmm – don't forget. I know what it's like to have to work with that man in a parish.'

There was a distinct place in the parish pecking order set aside for a deaconess. This became all too obvious at staff meetings. Donald was at the top, followed by his wife Rosemary. They in turn were followed by Stephen (and Tony eventually) and their wives. Then there were the churchwardens and treasurer who in Deignton, just happened to all be men. I brought up the rear, followed by Keith who, as one of the new breed of 'clergy husbands' hardly registered in the pecking order at all. As well as the close bond of priestly and potential priestly fellowship between my clergy colleagues, there was the impenetrable grip of the 'clergy wives' group, which was every bit as exclusive. This group, made up of full-time clergy wives and mothers, met every month in different vicarages. In and amongst the knitting, vicarage gossip and cups of tea, these women seemed to regard each other as somewhat different from all other wives, because of where they lived and what their husbands did. Many were keen to remind me from time to time of the stresses and strains of having to live in a vicarage. However, I often suspected that other less privileged wives wouldn't have minded exchanging their crippling monthly mortgages for life in a large, maintained, rent and rate-free house with a husband who worked from home and was occasionally available in the day to look after the children.

One day, whilst browsing through the church magazine, Keith decided to give himself a higher profile within the parish pecking order. He suddenly looked up and announced, 'Right, that's it. Clergy wives. I'm going to join the clergy wives group. Says here that they're having a retreat. Well, I'm a sort of clergy wife. I've waited long enough for *them* to invite me. So I think I'll go and invite myself.'

Donald's wife was not quite sure about Keith's request to join their retreat. This delicate matter was raised with me at the staff meeting the following week. As Rosemary entered the room with a rattling tray of cups and saucers, she inquired of me, 'Has Keith said any more about joining the clergy wives? It's just that a few of us have been talking about him joining us, but . . . well we don't really know . . . we've never had a man before.'

Amidst everyone's polite laughter, I smiled and replied, 'Well, he is fairly respectable and he's definitely house-trained. You never know, he might be just what you need.'

The laughter subsided and she continued, 'Yes . . . er . . . well, it's not that really. It's just that at times we like to talk about . . . women's matters, and . . . well, we couldn't then, could we . . . I mean he wouldn't be interested.'

'I don't know . . . he might be.'

'Well, that's the other thing I wanted to say. This retreat, we're all women and, as I say, we've never had a man before. He'll be the only one . . . he won't want to be the only one, will he?' She fixed a desperate gaze on me but I didn't respond. 'Then there's the question of bedrooms, you see. Where will he sleep? Where will we put him?' She continued to almost plead with me. 'The thing is . . .' (she hesitated to say this, and looked at Donald apologetically before doing so) 'we like to gossip sometimes as well. I'm sure Keith wouldn't want to listen to a lot of wives doing that, would he?'

'Oh, I think he would, actually. That's one of the reasons he wants to join . . . to keep up to date with vicarage news and gossip.'

'Then there's the question of transport. Our husbands take and fetch us, and I know all the seats are taken.'

'That's no problem. Keith will be taking his own car. He can give you a lift if you like, Rosemary, and save Donald a job, if you think that would help.'

I knew that this just wasn't the answer she wanted to hear. On hearing my cheery suggestion and seeing the increasing desperation in his wife's eyes, Donald decided to intervene.

'Never mind, dear, I'm sure that Jill will give it all some thought, if you leave the matter with her.'

Rosemary took this as her cue to leave. She offered me a resigned smile, raised her eyebrows at Donald, and with tea tray in hand, left the room.

Realising that this was a somewhat delicate area, I'd no wish to be insensitive. So when Rosemary and I happened to bump into each other the next day in the market, I decided to broach the subject with her again.

'About yesterday, Rosemary, and the clergy wives. Keith would really like to go on that retreat. You see, he supports me just as you support Donald, and he, like you, needs to be involved and included and supported. As you say, that's what the clergy wives group is all about. I know all this is new, and a bit uncomfortable . . . for you and for us, but if we try, we can work through it, can't we?'

She smiled. 'Funnily enough, that's just what Donald said as well last night.'

'Well, there you are then. It must be right if Donald's said it. Donald's always right!'

We laughed, and she then went on to explain further. 'It's not Keith, you know. I hope you don't think that. It's just that he's a man, and he's the first one, and we've never . . . you know . . .'

'I know.'

We started going our separate ways, but as I took my place in the cheese queue, she came back and tapped me on the shoulder.

'You think on. Donald's not always right about everything, you know. You'll do well to remember that.'

All this talk of women's roles and men's roles in the clergy team brought into sharp focus the responsibilities which men and women in the congregation undertook in Deignton. The men were charged with the 'business' of the church. This included the leading of worship, the finances, chairing the many meetings and so much more. The women's contribution seemed to be confined to the 'caring' side of church life. After permission from the clergy (or sometimes their wives), the women were allowed to clean, cater, look after, or visit, but they were always accountable to the priests and their wives. It was against this background that I struggled to assert myself in professional parish ministry. I was always being encouraged by Donald to confine my work in the parish to women and children. Some women took their lead from the clergy too in this matter, and they asked me such things as:

'Would you like to join us on the tea rota?'

'Are you coming to help us in the crèche?'

'The ladies take it in turn to clean the church hall every week . . . you'd be very welcome.'

All this was very well meant. None of these jobs was beneath me. I did most of them every day at home. However, it was important that if deaconesses were to pave the way for women priests in the years to come, then women like me must be seen to have a broad range of abilities in ministry. Only then would we ever begin to blur the edges of difference between what had come to be the accepted roles of men's and women's ministry within the Church. So I learnt to answer these friendly requests with a cheery smile and a question.

'Oh, have you invited Donald and Stephen to help too?'

'Oh no, we don't ask them. We just asked you because . . . well, you're sort of like one of us, aren't you?'

'Thank you. It's lovely to be one of you. But the thing is, you've got to remember that I'm also one of them as well, so I'll have to say no.'

Even at the Clergy Chapter meetings I would receive invitations to stay in the kitchen. Sometimes I felt like accepting! These meetings could be so dull and tedious. Chapter meetings for the clergy of the area took place in a different vicarage on one morning every month. Parish events and issues were discussed, and as the only woman in the deanery, I often felt like a fish out of water in a room with all these elderly male clerics. One month I just happened to be a few minutes late for the meeting. Mrs Oglethorpe ushered me in at the kitchen door. Her son, Frank, was vicar of a semi-rural parish nearby. Frank was of indeterminate age, unmarried, extremely old-fashioned and painfully shy. In fact, when I first met Frank, I had assumed that Mrs Oglethorpe was his wife.

As she took my coat and scarf she assured me, 'Don't worry, they've only just started. Although why you want to sit in a room with that miserable lot beats me. You'd be better off helping me make the coffee. Keep your gloves – you'll probably need them in there. Let's see what they're getting up to. Look, you can see for yourself if you peep through here. This is what I do.'

She steered me along the corridor to the door of her son's study, which was a tiny bit ajar. There was a crack in this heavy wooden door, and through it we peered into the large room. I could see all my colleagues sitting in what seemed like a sombre silence. I whispered across at her, 'Do you think they're saying the opening prayer?'

She shook her head back at me in a knowing sort of way, and whispered, 'Nah . . . shouldn't think so. They always look like that.'

Through stifled giggles we made our way back into the kitchen, where she continued, 'I tell you, they're an odd lot. There's one of them in there he'll eat every biscuit you put in front of him. Then there's that one who always looks as if he's slept in his clothes. Funniest one though is that vicar from Alstable . . . Harold . . . that's him. You must have seen him . . . waterproof trousers and his plastic raincoat on, inside and outside, winter and summer. He'll never let me take that raincoat off him and hang it up you know, when he comes here. Ooh no. If you ask me he must be ready basted under all that. He's got it on today . . . you'll see him when you go in. Frank says even when he's sat with his eyes closed in church on those clergy quiet days they have, he can always tell where Harold's sitting because he can hear him rustling about. They are an odd bunch and no mistake. What do you want to mess with them for?'

I tried to stifle my giggles and compose myself by turning to look out of the window, but she came to join me again which didn't help.

Nodding towards the graveyard she went on, 'I tell you there's more life out there than there is in that study. Do you know, I got told off last time they came here, for having my radio on. Can you believe it? One of them wanders out here and says "We're finding it somewhat distracting . . . do you mind?" Does no more than switches it off. My own radio in my own kitchen!'

We were both doubled up by this stage. I tried for a second time to compose myself. I closed my eyes, took a deep breath, walked purposefully towards the study door and almost succeeded. Then once again, my giggles got the better of me and I had to stagger back into the kitchen.

Eventually I told her, 'Look, it's no use, Mrs Oglethorpe, I'm going to have to go in. I'll see you at coffee time.' With tongue in cheek I mouthed back at her, 'And don't go making too much noise. We don't want disturbing, you know.'

She whispered back at me, 'Trouble is, love, I think that's just what some of 'em do want! Good luck – rather you than me.'

I walked in, made my hasty apologies and took my place on the one vacant upright chair, which was in front of a full-length, draughty sash window. Fifteen elderly black-suited, prayerful vicars were discussing the venue for the next deanery quiet day and the archdeacon's visitation. I had walked into another world. I wished I'd stayed in the kitchen!

7

Arrivals and departures

Strange how sometimes with hindsight a seemingly inappropriate question at an interview can turn out to be the most pertinent and prophetic.

'What will you wear in the parish?' Donald had asked me that day at my interview.

'Silly man,' I'd thought at the time. 'What does that matter?'

Actually it mattered quite a lot. He was right to ask it. I soon discovered that not looking the part was the root cause of much frustration as a young deaconess.

Many a time I was sent to visit the likes of Mrs Reid. She was one of the many frail, elderly people living in sheltered accommodation in our parish. There I would be on the doorstep ringing the bell. I could see her net curtains twitch as she eyed me up suspiciously through the side window. Then slowly she would make her way to the front door and call out.

'Who are you? I'm not buying anything.'

'I've come from the church, Mrs Reid . . . from St Philip's. I'm the deaconess.'

'Yer what? What's one of those?'

'One of these,' I would call back, and in a vain attempt to convince her of my authority (such as it was) I would dangle my big deaconess' silver cross, which I always wore on a long chain around my neck, through her letter box.

Moments later, I would nearly be garrotted, as with failing eyesight she would pull the cross towards her to get a better look at my credentials. Then, opening the door just a fraction, she'd peer out. By this time I would have retrieved my cross and have just about regained consciousness. Still, she would not be convinced of my identity.

'A deaconess? Well, you don't look like one, do you? Haven't you got a uniform or something?'

I'd wilt inside. Why hadn't I taken Donald's advice at the interview and bought myself that nice navy blue crimplene suit that retired missionaries wore? I'd try again to win her confidence.

'Well, I do wear special clothes in church, Mrs Reid, but just ordinary clothes outside. I always wear this cross though. It's a special one that only deaconesses wear.'

'Well, I can't see that under your coat, can I? What do you want? It's Father Stephen who I see. I like him. Does he know you're coming? Anyway, you can come in if you want. You might as well, now you've had me opening this door. It sticks, you know.'

Welcomes like this were not uncommon. I'd chuckle to myself many a time in staff meetings when Donald shared with us the odd occasion when he felt that a parishioner had slighted him and not treated him with what Donald considered to be due deference and dignity befitting a man of his station.

'Try being a deaconess for a day,' I'd think to myself, 'you'll soon get used to it!'

There had been a time when I used to think that not being able to drive around the parish would be a hindrance. I soon found out that it was an asset. I seemed better placed to be able to reach those parts of the parish that other more mobile clergy did not reach. Admittedly, queuing for buses and wandering round on foot did take time, but it really was the best way of getting to know people. I could glean more pastoral information waiting for the 245 bus from town every teatime, than I ever could over coffee after church on a Sunday.

It wasn't just the information people offered me in conversation, but the overheard snippets of other people's conversations, which, if you're nosey like me, you just couldn't help but overhear. There I was one day with my shopping and three children squashed onto a bus seat, and there were two women talking behind me.

'Shame about Arthur Pickup, isn't it? He'd only just made eighty, you know. Saw him out gardening that morning too . . . well I would, do you see . . . he only lived five doors down from me.'

'What's his wife called again? Evelyn . . . that's it. How's she taken it all?'

'Huh! Well you know what *she's* like. To look at her you'd think her and him had been devoted . . . floods of tears, can't cope. Mind you, she doesn't fool me. She's led Arthur a right dance all these years. Gallivanting here, there and everywhere. They tell me she's still seeing that Frank you know, and it seems he knew all about it, did Arthur. No, I don't think *she'll* ever change. Anyway, this is my stop, Betty . . . I'll see you later.'

Invaluable little snippets like that shed a whole new light onto my task the following day. At three thirty I would be on duty at Deignton Crematorium, officiating at the funeral of Mr Arthur Pickup. 'Will Frank be there?' I asked myself.

As a deaconess I took lots of funerals. It was something we were actually allowed to do by ourselves. We had three undertakers in Deignton, but Peter Crosland was the main one. I soon became used to sitting in hearses, either in the front seat next to the driver, or in the little fold down seat in the back next to the corpse. Undertakers and their drivers were always wonderful sources of funny stories. The first time I met Peter he was driving and I was in the back next to the coffin. It was a sunny day and there was a speck of dust in my contact lens and so my eye was watering. Peter spotted my predicament in his mirror.

I was carefully dabbing my eye with a tissue when Peter asked, 'Are you all right?'

'Yes, I'm OK thanks. It's just my contact lens.'

'I thought you were in tears then. I was just going to tell you to keep it up . . . it's good for business!'

Every undertaker had a funeral that stuck in the memory, and Peter was no exception. He told me a tale of when his father was still in charge of the business. It was a very foggy day. Peter and his father were in the hearse, wearing full funeral regalia. Peter was driving, and there were two other funeral cars behind him full of mourners. The burial was at an out-of-the-way country churchyard. Peter's father had been to see where the grave was a few days earlier, and had arranged the preparation of it. On the day of the funeral, as the hearse and cars turned off the main road and onto the country lane, Peter's father had got out of the hearse. He proceeded to walk ahead of the cars in his top hat and tails leading the procession to the graveside. Peter was driving the hearse, but it was so foggy that he lost sight of his father walking ahead. Evidently as Peter's father turned left into the cemetery, the hearse and all the other cars turned right into a boggy field and got stuck.

Etiquette was difficult in a hearse. If I saw one of my friends, should I smile and wave, nod and acknowledge, or just pretend not to see? I never knew. But it was a serious business burying the dead, and it was important to be able to remain detached and professional during a funeral. There could be distractions. For instance, how many hearses get stopped at traffic lights by a kangaroo? Ours did. It was Red Nose Day and we were on the way to the crematorium. As the hearse pulled up at the traffic lights, a kangaroo banged on the driver's window and waved a bucket at the driver.

The driver turned to me and said, 'Would you avert your ears a moment please, ma'am.' Undertakers often called deaconesses 'ma'am'.

I pretended to do so out of politeness, but I purposely kept my ears sufficiently uncovered to hear what the driver was saying. He wound down his window and gave this human kangaroo a mouthful of unrepeatable expletives, a two-fingered hand gesture and we drove off.

'Sorry about that, ma'am. There's a time and a place, and people like that . . . well, they need telling.'

Peter's son Paul was in his late teens. He often picked me up from home in the hearse to take me to a funeral. He always came round and opened the car door for me. In I got with my robes and case. As soon as he closed his driver's door, he switched on Radio One at full volume and bopped along until we were approaching the house of the deceased's family. Then he'd switch off the radio and resume normal funereal behaviour. Hours later, I'd get back home to be greeted by Tom, Rachel and Julie.

'Mummy, we saw you sitting in that car with all those flowers. Why didn't you wave to us when we waved to you?'

That's what I mean – hearse etiquette . . . what do you do?

In such a large parish like ours we could have up to eight funerals a week – sometimes more. So there were plenty to go round between two curates, a vicar and a deaconess. All funerals demanded time, care, tact, concentration and a lot of love. Whether I'd known the deceased person, or, as was more often the case, whether I'd not, my role was to try and reflect something back to the deceased's family and friends of how much that person was loved and how much they mattered – and of course, how much they were valued by God. All funerals were poignant. Some funerals were amusing.

Raymond, who drove for the Co-op, liked to tell me about the time when the officiating priest died 'on the job' so to speak . . . actually in the hearse on the way to the crematorium. Raymond didn't notice that anything was wrong with him until he turned off his engine and was getting out. There were all the mourners waiting outside the crematorium for the hearse to arrive, and there was the officiating vicar sitting dead in the passenger seat. Raymond discreetly told the undertaker and they telephoned for an ambulance. The mourners were ushered into the waiting room and told that the vicar has been taken ill.

'One minute,' said Raymond, 'there we were talking . . . you know, just like you and me. I thought he'd gone a bit quiet then, but I didn't think anything of it till we stopped. Every time I pull up here now, I think of him. It just goes to show . . . you just never know, do you? What a place to die though . . . in't hearse.'

Mrs Florrie White was my first funeral. She was eighty-seven and I actually knew her. I'd taken home Communion to her in a little sitting room-cum-bedroom. It was a ramshackle little room with threadbare curtains that didn't meet in the middle. Florrie lived in her own house, which looked out onto bleak moorland. She was confined to this one room, which boasted an old double bed, a gas fire, a commode, a shabby easy chair, and a terrific draft blowing under the door from the cellar. Her legs were in a sorry state, but Florrie could just about hobble to the kitchen on a good day. The kitchen was tiny, dark and dingy with a dirty old chip pan on an even more ancient gas ring. Florrie and I had had a long conversation after our home Communion service about her only son, Alan. Florrie's husband had been killed in a mining accident when Alan was two, and with very little money she had brought him up single-handed. All round the room there were photographs of Alan. He was the apple of her eye, her pride and joy. Alan had married a Canadian lady, settled in Canada and now had two daughters aged fourteen and twelve. Florrie wrote to Alan nearly every week without fail, despite her arthritic hands. It was a mammoth effort for her to put pen to paper and then manage to get it in the envelope. She couldn't get out to post it, but a kind friend would often do this for her. Sometimes Alan wrote back. His letters were kept in an old chocolate box and tied up with a blue ribbon. This box was her most treasured possession. Florrie hadn't seen Alan since he'd emigrated fifteen years before, but her face had lit up when she'd spoken of him to me.

'One day,' she told me, 'I'll be able to go out and see him . . . you know, see where he lives.' Her face had beamed. 'One day he's going to bring his wife and children to meet me, you know.'

Then she'd gone quiet and her face had crumpled before me as she had tried without success to fight back the tears. She'd gone on to tell me that a former neighbour of hers had bumped into an old school friend of Alan's in Deignton. Apparently, Florrie's grandchildren were being educated in England at a private school, and Alan and his family were frequent visitors to this friend's house.

Understandably, Florrie had been devastated to hear this news, and had told me, 'I don't suppose he wants them to see me having to live like this. Must be a bit ashamed of me now that he's moved up in the world. I'd give my eye-teeth to see him . . . just once more. Still I can dream can't I, and I've got my memories. I don't want anything from him. Just to see him again would be enough for me. He's everything to me is our Alan . . . always will be.'

On the day of Florrie's funeral, I was standing at the front of the church, leading the service. About thirty people had come to pay their last respects, and they were all scattered around the church. On the front pew sat Alan, his wife and both of their children. Alan was within touching distance of his mother's coffin. I announced the last hymn. It was the one that Florrie had chosen to be sung at her funeral. And as we were singing 'O love that will not let me go', Alan stepped forward and placed a single, red rose on his mother's coffin.

I watched him with a lump in my throat, and thought to myself, 'What your mother would have given to see you again in this life! She has given you everything she had, and her love for you has been constant. You may have influence and money now, but in her attitude towards you, your mother has shown you more about the love of God than you'll probably ever know. Poor Alan. Your mother is very rich in the eyes of God, and you've just failed to see it.'

Isn't it always the way of things? Just as I was beginning to get a bit of experience under my belt as far as funerals were concerned, and my confidence was growing, along came Mrs Ashworth to cut me down to size.

It was a dismal Sunday evening in May. I'd been on duty since eight o'clock in the morning, and it was now quarter past seven. I had sung, prayed and preached my way through four different services, as well as talking to umpteen people over tea and coffee after each one. I was ready to go home. The following day was my day off. Donald had given me a funeral to do on Wednesday morning, and I needed to do the funeral visit this evening if I wanted to have my day off . . . which I did. Tuesday had its own commitments, and in any case, I needed time to prepare my funeral talk for Wednesday.

I searched in my handbag for my diary to find the address. The deceased was a Mr Cedric Ashworth and the next of kin was his wife Betty, who was staying at her daughter's house. I roamed the country lanes looking for the address. The undertaker had told me that the house was just off the main road. After knocking at two doors by mistake, I realised that the house I was looking for was actually a cottage attached to and behind a house on the main road.

Tired and hungry, I stood on the doorstep and rang the bell. A middle-aged lady peered out at me from a side window, and then let me in. I was shown into a long, dark-beamed room with wooden floors and a lovely open fire. Here I was introduced to the redoubtable Mrs Ashworth. She was a thin, wiry, alert lady propped up on cushions as she reclined in an easy chair.

Sitting bolt upright as I entered the room, she accosted me with the words: 'I thought you weren't coming . . . still, never mind, you're here now.'

I walked across to her with my hand outstretched. 'I'm very pleased to meet you, Mrs Ashworth, and I'm so sorry to hear about your husband.'

She lurched forward at me in her chair. 'Are you? What for? It were expected.'

'Well, I'm sure it's still a shock for you, and I'm sorry that we have to meet under these circumstances.'

Over the next few minutes, I tried to encourage her to tell me about her husband. I asked her how he died, and what sort of a man he was. However, all this did not feature even remotely on Mrs Ashworth's agenda. My attempts at conversation only seemed to make her more exasperated.

'I'll tell you all about him later. First thing I want to do is choose t'hymns. It's been nattering me ever since he died, hasn't it, Beryl.'

Her daughter looked across at me, raised her eyes to heaven, and then closed them again. It was a look that said it all. I asked Beryl if she was an only child. She fixed her gaze on me, and there was so much tension and desperation in her one-word reply.

'Yes.'

'Are there any hymns in particular that you have in mind, Mrs Ashworth?'

'Well, that's what I want to talk to you about. What do you know? What do folk usually have?'

'"The Lord's My Shepherd" . . . that's one that's always popular.'

'Which one's that?' demanded Mrs Ashworth. 'You'll have to sing it for me. I don't think I know it.'

I burst into song and was nearly at the end of the first verse when Mrs Ashworth leant forward and stopped me mid-flow with a hand in the air and a derisory triumphant look on her face.

'Nay . . . that's same one Mrs Garside had for her Cyril.' She announced this as if it was a piece of information I should have known. 'I aren't having anything she's had. What else do you know?'

It had been a long day, and at this rate it could well have been a long night. My next melodic offering to Mrs Ashworth was 'Dear Lord and Father of Mankind'. I was instructed to sing it, but I was only on the second line when the hand went up again.

'Nay . . . Mrs Benson only had that last week at hers. We can't have that.'

'The trouble is, Mrs Ashworth, I don't actually know which hymns your neighbours have had.' Then suddenly I was inspired. 'What about "Amazing Grace?" Do you know that one?'

At the very mention of this hymn, Mrs Ashworth's face turned into a disgusted sneer.

'I do and it's common. We sang that at Bessie Sykes'. She were man-mad, that woman. We don't want reminding how amazing she was, thank you.'

Time was getting on and I could tell that this could well be a long session, so I tried to think of a more obscure hymn that none of her neighbours would have even thought of having for their funeral. In a flash it came to me.

'"Jesus Good Above All Other". What about that one?'

Mrs Ashworth stared at me in total silence for a few seconds, and then, finally stumped, said, 'Well, go on then . . . sing it for me.'

I warbled my way through the first verse as instructed, stopped and awaited a reaction. There was none. I was just breathing an inward sigh of relief, when she retorted, 'Don't you know any more?'

I dutifully started the second verse, and I stopped at the end of the third. My rendition was met with complete and utter silence. Then Mrs Ashworth delivered her verdict.

'That'll do, but I hope we aren't singing it that high on Wednesday.'

I offered her a weak smile. My audition now over with, she went on to tell me about herself.

'I don't come from round here, you know. I were born and bred in Symmington. I still have a lot of friends there . . . proper friends too. I've only got neighbours here . . . not what you'd call friends. I'm from Symmington, you see.'

'But how long have you lived here in Deignton, Mrs Ashworth?'

'Fifty-two years. Mind you, when I say neighbours, they're not like neighbours should be. There's a young couple next door to me, and you wouldn't believe what they get up to in their garden. They're partying till God knows what time. And they wear next to nothing, you know. Sometimes when you're pegging out your washing, you don't know where to look.'

After Mr Ashworth's funeral service in church on Wednesday morning, there we were in one of the funeral cars on our way to the cemetery. This journey could take anything from ten minutes to half an hour, depending on the trains. There was a level crossing between St Philip's and the local cemetery. Many a time half the mourners would be gathered at the graveside on the hill, waiting for the train to go past so that the rest of their funeral party could join them.

It was a boiling hot day. I was sitting in the front of the funeral car in a queue of traffic with Peter, the undertaker. In the back of the car were Mrs Ashworth, her daughter, and Mrs Ashworth's cousin who looked every bit as fierce and determined as Mrs Ashworth herself.

We were crawling along in the traffic, when out of the corner of my eye, I became aware of this cyclist pedalling alongside us. I had to stifle a giggle, because on inspection this man seemed not to have a stitch on. I did wonder if this was Mrs Ashworth's 'neighbour from hell' that she'd been telling me about the other day. If so, then he would appear to be having the last laugh. He positioned himself right in front of our funeral car. I could now see that he was wearing a very skimpy black leather thong. I daren't even glance at Peter, because I knew if I did, I might well give way to my giggles. We both tried hard to stare ahead professionally, but with two bare buttocks wobbling in front of you, it was difficult to look anywhere else.

I was just about keeping my composure, when I heard Mrs Ashworth complain to her daughter, 'I don't care how hot it is . . . it's disgusting. It shouldn't be allowed.'

And her cousin chimed in, 'Well, not near a cemetery anyway.'

It was only at this point that I nearly lost my composure and gave into my giggles. I couldn't quite understand why nudity within close proximity of a cemetery should be any worse or any better than nudity anywhere else. What with the nude cyclist and the warm weather, we were all hot and sticky when we got out of the funeral car at the cemetery. Everyone gathered round the grave. I said the words of committal, and then I stood back to give the family time to look at all the wreaths on the grass.

By this time, Mrs Ashworth was in full command of the situation once again, and demanded of her daughter, 'Who's sent that one over there? No, not that . . . that one in't middle. Bend down, Beryl, and have a look. Who's it from?'

Beryl dutifully bent down and reported back. 'It's from Aunty Violet, Mum.'

'Huh! I might have known. Well, that can't have cost her much . . . and she knows he never liked purple.'

I turned away and smiled. I somehow felt pleased for Cedric that he was now at peace. As I shook hands with the mourners, Beryl came across with her husband and son to thank me.

It somehow felt right to say to them, 'I do hope that it won't be too long before your mother is able to go back to her own house.'

Beryl and her husband exchanged desperate glances before replying, 'We all do.'

Three little words, said with such feeling.

8

Where do I belong?

What was it that a baby could do that a summer fete, countless bishop's initiatives, and even a new vicar, couldn't? Unite the parish – that's what. The body of a day-old baby girl had been found by an elderly couple from St Philip's in some woodland, just beyond the graveyard. Despite extensive inquiries, the police had not been able to trace the mother. This little girl's short life, and manner of her death, had touched and united the whole congregation and parish. As a congregation, we wanted to give her a funeral that offered her a dignity in death that she had not had in life, so first of all we decided to give her a name – Katherine. The church was packed for baby Katherine's funeral, with crowds of people outside in the graveyard too. The local press was there along with representatives from the police and health services. Two men from the congregation had made her coffin, and the ladies of the church had placed a little posy of buttercups and daisies on top of it, as her body had been found among those flowers. It seemed that everybody now owned this little girl. It was as if in death, she belonged to us all. Donald and Stephen were to lead the funeral service, and I was asked to give the address.

I chose my Bible reading with care. I asked Stephen to read about the time when Jesus healed the leper, and in doing so, gave the leper not just his freedom but a sense of dignity and the feeling of belonging in the community. Katherine's death reminded us that we belonged together. Although we couldn't physically heal her as Jesus did with the leper, we could restore her dignity and commend her to God as one of us. She was now a person who belonged, a person with a name and a person we would remember. Her tragic death had touched all of us, and brought us together. United in grief, this event had forced some people to put aside their own divisions and differences with each other. In this way Katherine's death had gone some way towards healing us as a community too.

This sad occasion reminded me that although women tended to be sidelined in the Church's professional ministry, deaconesses were allowed to stand on two very public platforms. Both of these platforms gave us a high profile in the Church and in the community. Firstly, we were allowed to preach. The sermon is usually the only said part of the main Sunday service (give or take a few prayers) which is different every week. The sermon is there to feed, affirm and challenge our faith. It should always capture, and sometimes amuse. Sadly, I had had enough experience of Church life to know that pious, aloof sermons simply fall on deaf ears. They only serve to reinforce the picture of a remote, humourless God who seems to have little to say and wants little to do with the lives of ordinary people. In the church where I served there had never been a woman in the pulpit. This meant that none of my clergy colleagues or their predecessors would ever have been a homemaker, wife or mother. They would never have known what it was like to carry and then be delivered of children. Most of them would not have had to shop, cook, feed and clean regularly for a family. And yet, over the years, these men in the pulpit had preached, and still do preach, to many such women who have been, and still are just that. This gave many of the women a distinct advantage in the pulpit. Our theological insights were often based on different human everyday experiences. We could use illustrations in our sermons which were very close to home for many people in the congregations. I knew that this was so, because people were often keen to tell me.

'We can understand you . . . you're more on our level.'

'When you put it across like that, it really made me think. I've never looked at it that way before.'

'I wouldn't mind having a chat with you sometime about what you said in your sermon this morning . . . it rang bells with me, you see.'

'Do you know, when you preach I always know I shall be going home with something to think about.'

Of course, the second public platform on which a deaconess was allowed to stand in a parish was the taking of funerals. As in baby Katherine's case, these services reached out to the community. I took lots of funerals, and I found them very rewarding. School assemblies and funerals – these were times when I was allowed to be seen 'on my own' in the parish. So, under Donald's guidance, and in consultation with head teachers and undertakers, I grew in confidence. I was known and recognised by many. And so, although it was all too easy to feel sidelined within the parish structures, outside in the community there seemed to be a ready and growing acceptance of my ministry as a deaconess as well as an increasing bafflement as to why I, and others like me, were not allowed to do more.

The feeling of belonging which baby Katherine's funeral had brought about in the community was in sharp contrast with the deanery meeting which took place later that day in the church hall. Clergy and church representatives from all the neighbouring parishes met to discuss at local level the whole issue of women and the priesthood. At the end of these discussions, there was to be a vote to see whether our deanery was in favour. I felt somewhat vulnerable and 'under the spotlight' as the one deaconess in the deanery. Although I knew that it was not the case, I still couldn't help feeling that the result of the vote might depend upon what people thought about me. I would have felt much more comfortable about this meeting if there had been a few more deaconesses in the deanery.

At the meeting we were asked to divide into two groups for the purposes of discussion. The clergy were to meet in one group, and the laity, which was the rest of us, was to form the other. As I was not, strictly speaking, a member of the clergy, I made my way to sit with this large group of laity. In his opening remarks, the chairman had already drawn everybody's attention to the fact that, as a deaconess, I seemed not to really belong to either group. This remark, which perhaps was well intentioned, had drawn sympathetic looks and polite laughter from the meeting, but really had not helped the situation.

Feeling neither fish nor fowl, I was just about to sit down with the group of laity when a lady in this group, who seemed to speak for all the rest, said, 'We know strictly speaking that you are one of us, Jill . . . but do you mind, just for tonight? I think it's better if . . . you see, some people might not feel free to say what they think, if you were to join us . . . do you see what I mean?'

Of course I could see what they meant, so feeling something of a nomad, I wandered across to the group of clergy who hadn't yet started their discussions.

I explained my predicament to one of my colleagues, only to be told by another, 'Well, you're certainly not one of us – not yet, anyway.'

Another chimed in: 'Not ever if I have my way.'

What it was to belong in a loving, caring Christian community! I gave up and took myself outside into the churchyard. There I spotted Eric crouched over the church path with his trowel. He spent hours keeping the path tidy and planting little flowers along the edge. Eric never actually went to church, but he kept the path clear for those people who did. It was as if he wanted to make it easier for them to come and do what he couldn't. He glanced up at me.

'What's to do? Have they thrown you out?'

Sighing, I replied, 'No, I suppose not, but it feels like it. I'm going back in later. What about you? Don't usually see you here in the evening.'

'Ah well, I thought I'd bring a few of my flowers to put on little Katherine's grave. Come on . . . I'll show you what I've been doing.'

We made our way over to the small mound of earth. There was a simple wooden cross and the posy of wild flowers. By the cross Eric had added a small stone jar full of flowers from his garden.

In between sighs and sniffs, he patted the mound of earth as he told me, 'Do you know, after all these years, Jill, I think I've found somewhere. Don't suppose there's anybody left to remember now, but Elsie and me, we had a baby once . . . a little girl. Only we never saw her . . . they took her away. They told me they could either save Elsie or the baby, and I had to choose. I couldn't face losing Elsie. But you know ever since then, she always blamed me, did Elsie. You see, they never let her see the baby, and she'd got it into her head that I had. I kept telling her that I'd never seen her . . . that they'd taken her away, but I don't think Elsie ever believed me . . . you know, that I hadn't seen her. She always thought that I was keeping something from her. We never got over it. Things were never the same between us after that. This little grave will mean a lot to me . . . would have meant a lot to Elsie as well . . . might have helped, you know, just to have somewhere . . .'

It was as if his grief had been on hold for all these years. It had taken an unknown death to bring it all into the present again. Crouched down by the grave, I placed my hand on top of his on the soil, as I thought what to say.

'Let's thank God, Eric, for short lives as well as long ones, and especially for your little daughter's life all those years ago . . . for all that she was and is and always will be to you and Elsie and to God. Let's hope that this little grave of Katherine's is a place where you can come and grieve, Eric . . . and begin again. Amen.'

Eric squeezed my hand in his. It wasn't a time to say any more. I stood up, and with a hand on his shoulder, I turned and left Eric to his tears and tending, and walked back towards the hall.

When I got there, I jumped up and tried to peer in through the windows to see what they were all doing. I felt like a naughty child who had been sent out of the classroom at school. Please God that by now it was time for the vote. With my ear pressed to the door, I detected the purposeful bustling of my fellow Christians moving about, so I wandered back in to be greeted by cheery remarks.

'We wondered where you'd gone . . . you didn't have to go outside you know. It's nothing personal.'

I reassured them with the words, 'Well, you all seemed to want to talk amongst yourselves, so I thought I might as well get some fresh air.'

As I went to cast my vote the chairman spotted me and came across.

'Jill, I didn't mean to imply in the meeting that you belonged to neither group. Of course I hope you know you're one of us.'

'Ah yes, but one of who? Now that you mention it, what you said didn't really help. It can be lonely and uncomfortable enough being the only deaconess – especially in a meeting like this. I don't think you needed to make light of it in front of everybody like you did.'

He smiled benignly at me. 'We've all got to make light of these things sometimes, Jill.'

'Yes, but I'm not sure that tonight was one of those times. Sometimes it's much easier to make light of this issue than address it, and tonight I thought that that's what we were here to do . . . address it.'

He wandered off, shrugging his shoulders. Perhaps I was turning into one of those awful, humourless women, but I didn't care. To feel isolated and excluded by one's fellow Christians in a church meeting was bad enough, but why should I always be expected to see the lighter side of this? It was a serious issue, and there was a sense in which I must be seen to take myself seriously at times if I expected others to do so too.

9

Organs and ashes

At last I was let off the lead. I was actually allowed out on my own to take evensong in a neighbouring parish. At first I somewhat foolishly thought that I'd been invited, until Donald made it crystal clear that this was not the case.

'I've tried everyone else, and there's only you left, so I'm afraid you'll have to go.'

Presumably this parish couldn't find a man, and they were desperate enough to have a woman, but I didn't care. It wasn't as if Donald couldn't spare me. Evensong in Deignton could be a bit of a cumbersome affair with about twenty or so parishioners at the back, a full choir and three clergy and me officiating at the front.

Glad to escape, I arrived at St James's, Ringston, on a wild, wet Sunday night at six o'clock. Ringston was a tiny hamlet with a few streets, a shop, a pub, and of course a church . . . St James's.

Keith had given me a lift and dropped me off at the gate. Battling against the wind and the rain, I darted up the church path in my cassock clutching my bag, white surplice, case and umbrella. Having pushed open the massive door, I was greeted by an elderly man with an arm full of hymn books. He eventually looked up at me and smirked.

'Evening . . . you're a bit younger than we thought you would be. They only told me this morning that we were going to have to have a woman tonight. I daresay it's you, is it?' Putting down his hymn books, he then introduced himself. 'Arthur Hetherington . . . that's me. Now . . . am I right? Is it you?'

'Yes, it's me. Pleased to meet you, Arthur.'

We shook hands and he continued, 'And they tell me you're married . . . how come? I didn't think nuns could get married.'

'I'm not a nun. I'm a deaconess.'

'A deaconess? Ah well . . . that'll explain it. Now, is this your first time? Is there anything you want me to show you?'

'I just need you to show me where the vestry is, please.'

'Right you are . . . follow me.'

I felt my way up the dimly lit church aisle, and suggested that we put some lights on. At my request there was a sharp intake of breath, and Arthur stopped dead in his tracks, turned and looked at me.

'Ten minutes before. That's when we put lights on here . . . no sooner . . . never any sooner . . . can't waste electric you see.' He walked on and then stopped again. 'I'm just thinking…where will you be preaching from?'

'From the pulpit, please.'

'Ah, now then . . . that could be a bit difficult. You see that's where our ladies have to keep all their cleaning stuff now. As long as you don't mind sharing it with a vacuum cleaner and a few bin bags…'

'No thank you, Arthur . . . in that case I'll preach from the lectern.'

'Right you are. Just as you like.'

Arthur knew every nook and cranny of this church and confidently made his way towards the vestry. I had to tread carefully through the darkness after him with my case, bag, surplice and dripping unbrella. When I tripped up one of the steps, he didn't turn round but he helpfully called back, 'Always catches people out, does that one. Never fails.'

We reached a heavy wooden door and, using all his strength, Arthur put his shoulder behind it, pushed it open, and showed me into a very damp, gritty vestry. Every surface in this dingy little room was covered in mildewed papers and books, and the walls were wet through and peeling. There was nowhere to put anything down, and no hook to hang anything on, so I asked Arthur if he could just point out where the service register was.

As he delved into one of the heavy desk drawers to begin the search, I remarked, 'Looks as if you've a bit of work to do in here, Arthur.'

'Ay . . . well, we can't do all this before we've had that organ seen to. We've had somebody in to look at these vestry walls only last week. He reckoned we could even have dry rot. Plaster's that damp you see. It's being eaten away . . . he reckons there could be millions of orgasms behind this desk alone.'

Hoping he meant organisms I smiled to myself, but I didn't say anything. He found the register for me and left me to get ready. Within minutes he was back. He had forgotten to impart some vital information, namely that we hadn't got an organist. The woman who usually played for them had had to go into hospital to have her baby. I had learnt from bitter experience that singing unaccompanied hymns at a sparsely attended evensong was not a good idea. Arthur seized on my offer to play the hymns for them.

'Two for the price of one eh? Organist as well. It's a bit temperamental our organ. I'll have to show you what to do.'

We both wandered out to the organ where I learnt that it was not so much a case of what to do, as what definitely not to do.

As he wiped away all the bits of plaster from the organ stool, he said, 'Now you're not one of them who plays too loud, are you? Trouble is, if you play too loud on this thing . . . t'ceiling'll fall down . . . and we don't want that. And you see that stop there . . . yes, that one . . . well, whatever you do, don't touch it. If you touch that stop, every single light in t'church'll go out.'

A few minutes later I was robed up, composed and ready in the vestry. At half past six on the dot, I was to take my place in the vicar's stall at the front of the church, and Arthur would then come forward and introduce me to the congregation before I began the service. At twenty-five to seven I was still in the vestry. I couldn't get out. The door wouldn't open. I put down my books and tugged and tugged at it, but it was no use. It was stuck, and so was I. Like a weak and feeble woman I started to knock, but the door was so damp and solid that this had little effect. At twenty to seven, Arthur decided to come and let me out, but only after reminding me that the vicars they usually had could always manage the door, but of course they'd never had a woman before. I offered him a weak smile as I walked straight past him and took my place at the front of the church. Arthur followed me to the front and began his introduction.

'We're very pleased tonight to welcome Deaconess Sparrow. I've just had to let her out, you know. She couldn't open that door.' There was much amusement as everybody seemed to know about 'that door'. 'Anyway, she's offered to play the organ for us as well tonight, and that reminds me . . . something else I've got to tell you. You know Susan, our organist is having a baby . . . well, her husband rang me this afternoon to say that he's had to take her into hospital to be seduced.'

Nobody else seemed to see the funny side of this, but I couldn't help but think that he was about nine months too late. What with all this talk of orgasms and seducing, we proceeded with the opening prayer for evensong. 'Father, we have erred and strayed' . . . Hadn't we just!

It was Holy Week – the week before Easter. I was so busy that I was almost meeting myself coming back! There were home Communions, funerals, special services during the days and evenings and children's activity days. All these had to be prepared, and there were sermons to write for the Easter services too. As well as all this, I had three young children on holiday from school to care for. There seemed to be no respite. Then it all became clear. I knew just what I needed. I needed what Donald, Stephen and Tony had all got – a clergy wife running the home. No wonder my colleagues all managed to appear so prayerful and unruffled! Perhaps I could if I walked into meals made, clothes washed and ironed, and children cared for. During this hectic Holy Week schedule, there had also been a very draining experience to cope with.

Peter the undertaker, rang and asked me if I could officiate at the funeral of a Mr Roger Bryson. This was a young man of twenty-five who had died suddenly. He gave me the date of birth and his address, and finished by saying, 'There's no next of kin . . . no one to visit.'

I put the phone down and thought, 'How can I take a funeral of a man nobody knows? There must be someone who knows him . . . a neighbour or something. I'll go and see.' I believe that a funeral service must reflect each person's individuality and uniqueness before God, so I needed to try and find someone who actually knew this man Roger. The following day, I found myself on the doorstep of Mr Bryson's neighbour. He was a young man in his thirties with a baby in his arms.

'Hello, I'm from the church. I just wondered if you could tell me anything about Mr Bryson?'

'Mr who?'

'Roger Bryson . . . you know, the young man who lives next door?'

'Oh him . . . is that what he's called? No, we don't know him . . . heard him moving around like, but we've never seen him. Why, what's matter? Has he died or something?'

A few days later on a cold wet afternoon in Holy Week, the undertaker and I, just the two of us, met at the crematorium. We waited . . . but there were no mourners. So eventually Peter and I made our way into the chapel. We then stood and commended to God a person who nobody wanted to know or remember. It was such a sad and poignant service, and one which I have never forgotten. Both of us were used to officiating at funerals where well-chosen words and music, families and friends were the order of the day. At the end of this service, we stood side by side in the silence of the crematorium and bowed our heads before Roger's coffin. A man of twenty-five had died, and no one cared. We dabbed our eyes. There was nothing more to say to each other, so we just shook hands, thanked each other, and went our separate ways.

This experience, whilst reducing me to tears, made me appreciate more than ever the fact that I belonged. I had roots in a loving family and in a community. It had taken a lonely funeral to help me realise that my demanding home life was a valuable asset and not in any way an obstacle.

I needed to 'change gear' before I went home, so I decided to go for a cup of tea in 'The Upper Crust' café in Deignton, before the long trek up the hill. A man of about thirty brushed past my table, and then, smiling, came back to me.

'Thought it was . . . it is you, isn't it . . . you're from St Philip's, aren't you? Hope you're still looking after my mother?'

I couldn't place this man at all. I knew he didn't go to church, so I had to ask him, 'Your mother? You'll have to remind me . . . I'm sorry.'

'My mother . . . you know, Violet Davison. She's there week in and week out in your church . . . never misses. You must have come across her by now.'

In my mind I was still at the crematorium, but I felt my way through this impromptu conversation with the cheery words, 'I'm sure I have. It's just that it's not always easy to put a name to everybody. But don't you worry, I'll look out for her.'

'You do that.' He walked off with a smirk on his face.

I paid my bill and made for the door. Violet Davison? I couldn't place her at all. She wasn't in the Mothers' Union, and I was sure she wasn't one of those elderly people at evensong. I wondered who she was. Stephen would know. I'd ask him when I saw him next.

To his credit, Stephen didn't laugh out loud straight away when I asked him about Violet. With a knowing smile he just said, 'Violet . . . ah well, she doesn't like to sit with everybody else you know. That's why you won't have seen her.'

'Well, where does she sit, then? Her son says she's here every week.'

Stephen began to laugh. 'Well, he's right I suppose. She *is* here every week . . . in a manner of speaking, anyway. Come on, I'll show you.'

I followed him out of the vestry, between the choir stalls and up to the high altar. He felt for the light on the wall. The altar was covered with a heavy brocade cloth that reached down to the floor. Stephen lifted it up, and I peered underneath it with him.

'That's where she is. I'll get her out.'

Onto the altar Stephen proudly placed a box of ashes, bearing the name, 'Violet Davison'. On closer inspection, there were about six other boxes of ashes under the altar too.

Stephen explained.

'Donald has a habit of doing this sometimes. If people can't decide what to do with their loved ones, they sort of get left here. We ought to start charging ground rent or something. You see he forgets about them, that's the trouble. Mind you, so do the relatives. I keep meaning to remind Donald that they're starting to stack up a bit now under here. Anyway, next time you see Violet's son, you can tell him that she's doing all right, but she's not getting out much these days. Tell him if he'd like to come and visit, or better still take her out, we'd be only too pleased.'

Donald was preoccupied at the moment. The church council meeting was drawing near, and there were not just decisions to make regarding finance, repairs and policy initiatives, but people issues too. Adrian was the newest member of the church council. He and his wife were recent members of St Philip's, having only moved into the area eighteen months before. They seemed sensible, intelligent people, but I knew that Donald had reservations about them for two reasons. Firstly, they would keep on telling people at St Philip's that they had both 'found God'.

Finding God seemed to make Adrian and his wife permanently cheerful, positive and enthusiastic about everything in church life. Their evangelical fervour could be
somewhat wearing, and even daunting for many regular
worshippers who had been coming to St Philip's for years.
Most people at St Philip's were the sort of people who had
always been quite happy to keep God at bay through the
weekly round of meetings, rotas and routines. It wasn't so
much that they hadn't found God, it was just that they'd
never really thought of looking for him. Donald's other
reservation about Adrian was the fact that he was a rela-
tionship counsellor. This irritated Donald immensely at
meetings, because Adrian had a tendency to probe. This in
turn encouraged other people to ask questions too. Issues
that usually had only warranted a simple 'those in favour'
or 'those against', were now subject to lengthy discussions. Donald's steely but gentle authority was being
undermined as Adrian enjoyed posing searching questions in a polite but persistent manner.

Help was at hand. Among the well-heeled, reticent
ladies and the retired businessmen on the church council, there was one ordinary local voice. It was that of
Sam. Sam did come to church occasionally, but Sam had
his own reason for being on the church council. He had
cut the church grass, man and boy for nearly fifty years.
The cure of souls might well be Donald's domain as
vicar of the parish, but the care of the lawnmower and
all things pertaining to the shed and the church grounds
were most definitely Sam's department.

Adrian had strolled unwittingly into Sam's controlled
little empire of the church grounds at the last church council meeting. As Donald had wearily inquired at the end of
the meeting whether there were items of 'any other business' Sam had blurted out, 'Ay . . . I have. I'd like to know
who it is that's been tampering with my lawnmower.'

Adrian had cheerfully but cautiously replied, 'Actually, Sam, I think it might have been me. The shed door was open the other Saturday when I was in the grounds, and the gravedigger said he thought it would be all right if I had a go . . . just to help, you know?'

Sam had taken a deep breath and glared at Adrian across the table. 'No, I don't know. All I know is this. You've made a right pig's ear of it. That lawnmower can be very temperamental . . . needs careful handling. It's a very delicately balanced machine, or at least it was till you got hold of it. When I walked into that shed last week and saw it, my heart sank. It were in a right state. I'm telling you this, lad, don't you go touching it again, or you'll have me to answer to. Is that clear?'

Sam's threat across the table had been met only with Adrian's polite, helpful unruffled expression. Adrian had observed Sam. Having observed, he'd leant forward and very calmly said, 'Sam, I do hear what you are saying, and I can sense that you are very angry. A lot of my work involves anger management, and I can see that you have something of an anger issue here. Perhaps you need to think about addressing this, and if I can be of any help, perhaps with counselling or . . .'

By this time, Sam had been on his feet and red in the face as he'd barked across at Adrian.

'Counselling! I'll give you counselling. Look here lad, you tamper with that lawnmower again, and you won't need counselling – you'll need surgery! Right?'

Donald had tried hard to diffuse the tension between them, and had then hastily drawn the meeting to a close. It had not been a positive note on which to end the meeting, and whilst Donald was not looking forward to a repeat performance, I knew that he'd been quietly pleased with Sam's outburst.

10

Hot under the collar

Donald had been in conversation with John the archdeacon, and also with Mrs Oglethorpe. Frank Oglethorpe from Basingthorpe parish had suffered a very severe stroke and was expected to be in hospital for many months. His mother had moved out of the vicarage to stay with her sister. I had been a deaconess for over three years by this stage, so the bishop asked the archdeacon to ask Donald to ask me to help 'look after' this neighbouring parish for a few months. Still working under Donald's authority, and alongside the churchwardens of the parish, I was to make sure that the appropriate services were supplied with visiting priests, conduct family services and funerals, attend and sometimes chair meetings, organise a weekly confirmation class in the vicarage, take school assemblies, and generally visit and be around. Unfortunate as the situation was, I seized this opportunity, as it offered me a tiny degree of autonomy, though still within the familiar secure staff team in Deignton.

I had been allocated Frank's study in Basingthorpe vicarage as my base, as there was no parish office and no church hall. It was a narrow, dark, book-lined room with two large sash windows at one end. Frank's desk was under one of the windows, which looked out onto the graveyard. Everything was exactly as Frank had left it, and at first I felt that it was not my place to move anything on his desk. I sat there and looked out and recalled my first meeting with Frank. It had been a snowy day and I had set off early so as to be there on time at Frank's vicarage for the Clergy Chapter meeting. I ended up arriving far too early. Mrs Oglethorpe had made us both a cup of coffee and shown me into this very room. Frank had been lost for words that day. There were a lot of clergy who found it difficult to make 'small talk', and were more comfortable with business and theological talk, but Frank had seemed comfortable with neither. Amidst the awkward silences and the rattling of teacups, I had tried in vain to make conversation about his parish or the weather, but my only response from him had been a shy smile or a hesitant one-word answer. I had come home that day thinking to myself, 'That poor man . . . how on earth does he survive in a parish?'

I decided to make Basingthorpe's primary school my first port of call, and so I arranged to meet the head teacher, Mrs Duffield. She showed me around the school and introduced me to the teachers and children. We had just come out of the last classroom and it was nearly playtime. As we walked down the corridor together some children of about five and six rushed up to us.

'Mrs Duffield, when's Mr Oggy coming back? We like Mr Oggy.'

I glanced across at Mrs Duffield. 'Who's Mr Oggy?'

She smiled back at me. 'Mr Oglethorpe . . . your predecessor, that's who. The children simply adore him. In fact, they only know him as Mr Oggy. That's what he likes them to call him. He's as daft as anything with them all. He makes them laugh, pulls funny faces, peeps round classroom doors, writes silly poems, crawls about on his hands and knees acting the fool with them, teaches them songs, tells them stories. They all look upon Mr Oggy as their friend. I don't know – it's as if that man just comes alive with children. I'm sorry to have to say it, but you've a lot to live up to.'

I thought back to my first meeting with Frank in his study that day. How utterly wrong I'd been. How wonderful that this tongue-tied and shy man had such a great gift among children . . . that he could come alive with them in a way he never could in a clergy meeting or among a group of adults. And how short-sighted and wrong of me to judge him on a first impression. I learnt important lessons in school that day which I have never forgotten. I learnt that the gifts God gives us are often hidden and not on display for all to see, and that great gifts can be housed in the most unlikely of people.

My days as a deaconess were coming to an end. The necessary legislation has been passed in 1985, which allowed women to be ordained as deacons. Whilst there were a few women who chose to remain as deaconesses, most in 1987 then had another ordination service ahead of them. For the first time, women were to be allowed to become deacons, and therefore members of the clergy. There was much excitement and preparation . . . and opposition. Most of the newspapers found it difficult to grasp what the difference was between a deacon and a deaconess, and so they resorted to making great play of the fact that these women would now look different. They would now be able to wear the clerical collar.

But there was a question mark over whether we should wear the clerical collar. For those people who were opposed to the ordination of women, the sight of a woman in a clerical shirt could be inflammatory, and insensitive to their feelings. With this in mind, a distinctive lapel cross was specially designed for non-liturgical wear among the new women deacons. Many of the deaconesses questioned why we should be treated differently to our male colleagues. A male deacon on his ordination would automatically wear a clerical collar. The introduction of the lapel cross seemed to indicate an underlying reluctance by the Church to recognise and own our new identity as women deacons alongside our male colleagues. There was much resentment about this issue among the women, and the opponents of women's ordination made great play over this with such comments as, 'This is what women are like, you see . . . only bothered about what they wear and what they look like. Is this the sort of Church you want? They don't seem to understand that ministry in Christ is not just about being recognised.'

Comments like these within the diocese and beyond were often uttered by those very clergy who seemed to live in their cassocks, and whose clerical collars appeared permanently welded to their necks morning, noon and night.

It was decided, however, that although the lapel cross should be relied upon for identification purposes, the use of the clerical collar would be a matter for personal discretion. This somewhat lukewarm decision at least allowed us to prepare for the ordination service, and acquire the necessary garments. This was far from straightforward. It was decided in the diocese that for the ordination service, each deaconess would need a black cassock, a surplice, a white deacon's stole, and a clerical shirt. There was one slight hurdle to overcome, however, and this came in the shape of the bishop's new assistant in the diocese. He had been discharged by the bishop to oversee the practicalities of this special ordination service. His name was Major Charles Fellworthy, an efficient military man who expected his words to be listened to and then acted upon. Discussion was not part of his agenda, and he simply failed to understand the significance of this ordination day for the women. For him, this ordination service in the cathedral was just another event on another day, whereas for the women it was so much more. Some of the elderly deaconesses had served the Church faithfully for many years. They and others had hoped and longed and prayed for this day. It was going to be a very special day in their lives. As deaconesses, many had been sidelined for so long in the Church. Some of us had had to provide for ourselves in ministry so far. Living in the areas where the bishop had licensed us, we had had to pay for our own housing and even in some cases our own robes and expenses of office. Now, as newly admitted members of the clergy, we were determined that we should not, at least, have to pay for our new robes. Major Charles arranged a meeting with us.

Our spokesperson was Beatrice. She was an imposing figure. Tall and stout, and towering over most of us, she had a pleasant smile and was quietly spoken. Beatrice was a sort of cross between Peggy Mount and Mrs Slocombe. She did not suffer fools of any variety and she was definitely not a woman to be trifled with. We were to discover that she was more than a match for Major Charles. After he had presented us with the outline of the ordination day itself, Beatrice spoke up.

'Major, there is an issue of our garments. As I'm sure you know, we shall all need a black cassock for this service in the cathedral as well as . . .' She was not allowed to even finish her sentence, because the Major interrupted her with a dismissive wave of his hand and the curt reply, 'Oh just send me a list of all your women's measurements, and I'll order a job lot.'

His dismissive attitude towards her was like a red rag to a bull. Beatrice stood. Drawing herself up to her full height – and width – and towering over Major Charles, she was like a ship in full sail. She took a deep breath and her voice was clipped, curt and to the point.

'Major, I don't know whether you've ever noticed . . . but we women . . . are a different shape to you men. We all go in . . . and out in different places, and some of us go more in and out than others. We shall therefore need . . . and expect, to be measured properly and fitted correctly for these garments.'

It was Beatrice's finest moment. Major Charles hastily scribbled a note on his pad, and a few days later we were all informed that each deaconess was to receive a grant. This would cover the cost of a black cassock, a white surplice, a white deacon's stole, and . . . the clerical shirt.

I used to think that it was only the Church of England that was still in the dark ages where women were concerned, but that was before I'd entered the world of the clerical outfitter.

These establishments seemed to be staffed entirely by men, which may be understandable given the fact that their customer base had up until then been mostly men. What amazed me was that most of these men did not seem to have any knowledge of a woman's shape. I wondered if any of them had mothers, sisters, wives, or girlfriends? I was handed a cassock to try on in the clerical outfitters. It was the correct length for my height, but obviously made for a man, so I said, 'Well, yes, it is the right length, but this is a man's cassock, isn't it?'

A young male assistant offered me a superior look and then informed me, 'There's no difference, madam. Men and women . . . they're all the same.'

'But it's a woman's cassock that I want, please. One that's shaped properly.'

'What do you mean, "shaped"? They're all the same shape, madam. That's the point.'

'But they're not *my* shape. I'd like one that is shaped at the bust and waist, with the buttons fastening on the woman's side.'

'You'll soon get used to fastening the buttons, and if you want one that fits your . . . erm . . . proportions . . .' (I think he meant bust) 'just buy a bigger size and we can arrange for the extra length to be cut off.'

'But it won't fit anywhere else then, will it?'

He sighed and stared out of the window in exasperation before informing me in a petulant sort of way, 'Of course, you can arrange to have one specially made, madam, but you will have to wait . . . and you'll have to be measured.'

I wasn't sure whether this latter statement was a threat or a promise, but he and I made our way to the counter where a Mr Price had to be called upon to deal with me. Mr Price was in the stockroom, and he was the man who took the measurements for cassocks. My unhelpful assistant must have already had a quiet word with him about this strange breed of humanity awaiting him in the shop, because Mr Price, an elderly black-suited man with a tape-measure and thick glasses, came out looking somewhat flustered and hot under the collar. By this time I had taken off my coat and was ready and waiting. There was a sort of stand-off between the two of us, as Mr Price clung onto the dark curtain that separated the shop from the stockroom. Aghast, he looked across at me as if I was some alien being. Then with trembling hands and a red face he came over to me and began to fumble with his tape-measure round my neck.

'I'm all thumbs today I'm afraid.' Then, having measured my 'proportions' twice just to make sure, he made his way further down to my waist saying, 'That's the trouble with you ladies. You are all so varied, you see.'

When he had finished, he took the piece of paper with my measurements on into the back room. His young, surly assistant was then sent out to fill in further details on the order form. Without even looking at me, he ticked his boxes.

'Now madam, you can have a breast pocket for your pens if you want . . . do you want one?' I declined. 'No? Right, that's no breast pocket then. What about an opening in the side to get into your trouser pocket . . . will you be wanting one of those?' Again I declined, by feebly reminding him that it was a woman's cassock. I paid my deposit and left with a mixture of despair and hope that things wouldn't always be like this . . . please?

With this experience very much in mind, I decided to buy my clerical shirt elsewhere. There was a large branch of a very well-known clerical outfitters some miles away, so I decided to go there. I didn't hold out much hope of a more positive experience, as I discovered that most deaconesses had had their 'buying the first clerical shirt moment.'

Mavis, one of our more well-endowed colleagues, had been standing with her arms outstretched in the clerical outfitters, being measured by a young, flustered male assistant. As he had reached round the back of her with his tape-measure, her bra had come undone. Mavis had adjusted herself quickly, and had tried to make light of it, but this young assistant had been so upset by this experience, that he had had to be escorted into the back room by his colleague, and then sent for an early lunch.

I asked Keith to come with me to buy my clerical shirt. With a man at my side, perhaps I would fare better. We found the shop, which was actually below ground level. As we walked along the pavement, it was possible to see

right down into the shop. It was full of rows of black garments, and there was an elderly priest trying on a black
overcoat. A portly assistant with a tape-measure round
his neck was helping him. Keith and I looked at each
other, took a deep breath and walked down the stairs
into the shop. All the clerical shirts were on a rail under
the window so we walked across and began to look.
They were all men's shirts. Eventually the portly assistant pushed his way through the rails of garments and
addressed Keith.

'May I help you, sir?'

'It's my wife, actually. She needs a clerical shirt.'

His helpful expression immediately changed. He
closed his eyes, gave a slight shudder, winced, and then
stared at me in a withering, scornful way. It was as if I
had in some way infected his shop. Without saying a
word, he drew back a curtain above the rail of shirts. He
held back the curtain whilst we read the printed sign
behind it. The card on the window sill read:

> Items for females are not on display as these may
> offend some of our male customers. Please ask at the
> counter.

The curtain fell back and he walked away. He had not
said a word to me. Keith and I looked at each other. The
ordination was in three weeks' time. I had to buy a shirt.
Undeterred, I made my way to the counter and waited.
Eventually this same assistant came and stood pomp-
ously behind it. I began to explain.

'I need a clerical shirt. Have you got one I could look
at, please?'

'No.'

'Have you got a picture of one that I could look at?'

'No.'

'Well, I do need one, and I need one in three weeks' time.'

This man then bent down behind the counter, scrabbled about, and then, standing upright, placed on the counter a cardboard sign on a stand with numbers on it. He assumed this sign was self-explanatory, but it wasn't, so I asked him, 'What is it?'

Again without saying a word, he lifted up a fold-down flap at the top of the cardboard sign that read

Neck Bust Measurements For Female Deacons.

Immediately after I'd read this, he folded the flap down again. Perhaps the very sight of these words might offend the one priest in the shop who was still trying on countless black overcoats. I was still confused and baffled by this sign, so I tried again.

'What do I have to do?'

It was only then that he deigned to speak to me. His superior voice informed me, 'Madam, you measure your neck, and from that measurement, this chart will then be able to ascertain your individual requirements.'

In other words, the size of my neck should tell me how big my bust was. I looked at Keith and he looked at me. We'd had enough by this time, and we tried hard not to laugh. I couldn't help thinking, 'It's never like this in Marks and Spencer.' I asked to borrow my portly assistant's tape-measure and Keith measured my neck – thirteen and a half inches. We then scoured the numbers on the chart, only to discover that if I had a neck of thirteen and a half inches, then I should have a forty-inch bust. We concluded that whoever had made out this chart must have had a vivid imagination. Although my first clerical shirt fitted me perfectly at the neck, as for the rest of it, Keith always said that there was 'plenty room for improvement'.

The ordination day was wonderful. Our ordination retreat was some miles away, and none of us had seen our friends and families for four days. On the morning of the ordination service, there was great excitement as we all went down to breakfast wearing our clerical shirts for the first time ever in the history of the Church of England. We posed together on the staircase for a group photograph, and ate our breakfasts whilst being interviewed by people from radio and television. A bus arrived to take us, our luggage and robes to the cathedral where people were beginning to gather inside and out. As the bus drew in to the cathedral close, we were pointed at and photographed.

A senior person in the diocese had said to me some time ago that once women were seen in clerical collars, then the process towards priesthood would be inevitable. I had doubted him then, but as we walked through the crowds into the cathedral, I began to think differently. I could tell that people were not just looking at us as we were, but also as we could be (and, as some would have said, should be). As soon-to-be members of the clergy, we had already sworn our oaths of allegiance to the Queen, before our ordination rehearsal some days before.

After we had put on our robes and received last-minute instructions, the crucifer – the person who carries the processional cross, and a senior member of the cathedral staff came to say the vestry prayer. The sight of all these women before them in clerical dress for the first time clearly moved these men. They looked at each other and told us that they were delighted, proud, and humbled to be part of this momentous occasion in the history of the Church. We were then led out by the crucifer into a packed cathedral as people stood to sing the first hymn. Not only did the congregation look so pleased, but there was such an air of excitement about the whole occasion. Among the hundreds of people there, I still managed to spot certain people I had known from various churches over the years, and even from childhood. As we reached the point in the service where we were to be ordained, there was a hushed silence as the bishop laid his hands on each of our heads in turn. The bishop handed me a Bible. The archdeacon then took my deacon's stole and placed it over my right shoulder, tying it at my side. We then turned and faced the congregation to the sound of rapturous spontaneous applause. At the end of the service, the bishop led all the new women deacons down the main aisle to what must surely have been the longest hymn in the book. In such a vast building, by the time we got to the west door, we were so far away from the congregation that we were singing at least one verse ahead of them.

As we reached the fresh air and realised this, the bishop turned to us all and said, 'Never mind all that lot . . . they'll catch up eventually.'

Those few little words of his caused much amusement. He was referring to the huge congregation, but the women realised that his words could well be applied to the Church at large. Then after photographs, the bishop's reception, crowds, sunshine, cards, presents and flowers, along with our families and friends we eventually wended our way back home. The celebrations were far from over. The following Sunday, there was to be a parish lunch and reception in the church hall after the morning service for the congregations of Basingthorpe and Deignton. Few of the congregation had been able to get tickets for the ordination service itself, so they had to have their day too. There seemed to be a mixture of pride, delight and bemusement at the sight of me in a clerical collar, although I'm sure that there were reservations too for some. The fact that I was not allowed to do anything more as a deacon in the Sunday service than I had been doing as a deaconess didn't seem to concern them at all. The senior person in the diocese had been right – it was the collar. It, and I, among these people, were somehow visible proof that the Church had changed, and with an ordained woman in their parish there seemed to be an overwhelming feeling of pride that their church was right in the forefront of that change.

Stephen was firmly opposed to the ordination of women. However, as we shared the same sense of humour and got on so well, we kept forgetting about our different viewpoints on this matter. He was a wonderful friend and colleague and his wife Alison was an absolute godsend. Every parish should have an Alison. She was packed full of common sense. After my first Sunday morning service as a deacon, Alison, who was a very good photographer, made her presence felt at the back of church. Wearing my clerical collar, my long white cassock alb and deacon's stole, she took countless pictures of me on my own, and with Keith and the children. Then she spotted her husband coming across.

'Come on, Stephen . . . you as well. Let's have you next to Jill. I want to see you both together.' She saw Stephen and I exchange unsure looks about this suggestion. He wasn't comfortable with it and Alison knew why. She completely ignored him and battled on undeterred, pushing Stephen into place.

'Never mind about how you feel about women in dog collars. You've all day tomorrow to pray and witter on about that. All you have to do for now is stand there. This is Jill's day. You can save your words for later. Anyway, what about that picture you've got up in your study – Jesus with that prostitute? You don't mind looking at that, do you? If he can do that for her, then you can do this for Jill. There's no difference. Well, there is, I know . . . sorry Jill . . . I didn't mean . . . no offence. Wipe that miserable holy look off your face, Stephen. Anybody'd think you were going to a church meeting. Get your arm round her . . . cheese everybody . . .' Stephen gave in and we all ended up laughing. 'That's more like it . . . hold it there you two. That'll do . . . right.'

I decided to buy a frame for one of Alison's pictures. It was one of Keith and me together. This photograph had pride of place on the bookshelf on the landing. There I was in my white cassock, alb and green deacon's stole with Keith by my side.

Still feeling on a high after the ordination, I was soon cut down to size by a comment from Daniel, my neighbour's little boy. Daniel was six and though neither he nor his family had anything to do with church he sometimes came round to see Tom after school. One day whilst I was cooking the meal, Daniel came into the kitchen having just been upstairs. I had my back to him at the cooker as he came into the kitchen and inquired, 'Aunty Jill, you know that photo on the landing . . .'

'Yes.'

'Well . . . is it you?'

I felt so pleased that he had noticed it, and proudly answered, 'Yes, it is.'

Daniel remained standing behind me and said nothing, so I turned round to look at him. He had his head on one side and he was looking me up and down in a puzzled sort of way, so I said again, 'Yes, it is me, Daniel. Why do you ask?'

He breathed a big sigh, and with admiration exclaimed: 'Phew! I never knew you did karate.'

There is nothing like a child to bring you down to earth with a bump. But my karate ordination picture continued to make me smile, for it reminded me that I and other women deacons still had battles ahead. We'd not completed the journey . . . only begun it.

11

What a difference a day makes

No more standing on doorsteps, or shouting through letter boxes for me. Parish life was so much easier in a clerical collar! Doors opened. People smiled politely at me in shops and on buses. No longer did I have to scout round and beg my fellow clergy to come across to Basingthorpe to conduct weddings on already busy Saturdays in their own parishes. I was allowed to do them myself – but there was some initial opposition. I had come across such opposition when as a deaconess I first took funerals. My first funeral visit entailed standing on a doorstep and having the door closed in my face after being told by a man whose brother had just died, 'My brother would not want burying by a woman. Goodbye.'

Donald had known the family and had taken me straight back to the house after I'd made him aware of the situation. This time on the doorstep, Donald had stood firm and made it crystal clear to the brother: 'This woman is on my staff. She is a deaconess, and she is as well qualified as I am to conduct your brother's funeral. If you will not allow her to do so, then your brother will just have to stay on top, because there's nobody else going to be burying him in my parish.'

If women deacons were to become established, it was essential that, in a similar way, fellow clergy had to stand firm where weddings were concerned. If people were given a choice as to who was to conduct the wedding, the chances were that they would always choose a man because that was the way it had always been. My first wedding attracted much publicity on local radio and television, but the bride was only too pleased about this. Some time later, as I was just getting into my stride, I received a phone call from an irate bride's mother one night.

'I'm June Halton. We haven't met, but I believe that you're going to be marrying my daughter and future son-in-law. Is that right?' I confirmed that this was so and she continued, 'Well, I just want you to know that you are going to ruin my daughter's wedding day for her father and me. Is there no man available? Why are we not allowed to being our own priest with us?'

The wedding couple, whom I did marry eventually, were delightful, and had no objection whatsoever, but they were clearly embarrassed by their parents' reaction. I decided to speak to Donald about it. He urged me to stand firm, but suggested that I offer to meet with the parents before the day. This I duly did. They were not local people. The mother was the spokesperson, and she was emotional and angry. The father seemed well aware of church structures, and was aloof and rude to me in his approach. I was surprised to discover that he was a churchwarden at his local church. He referred sarcastically to the days before the ordination of women.

'Of course, that was in the days before they let your kind in. There'll be no stopping you lot now, will there?'

I didn't like his manner towards me, and I told him so, but he just leant forward and smirked.

'Well then, you'll just have to get used to it, love, won't you, because there's plenty more feel as we do . . . and our vicar's one of them.'

I had seen so many clergy bow and scrape and fall over themselves with respect for each other at meetings and church services, and yet I have seen some of these very same clergy refuse to even acknowledge and accord even a modicum of respect to the women deacons. This man's attitude towards me seemed to encapsulate much of their scorn and ridicule too towards 'people like me'. Both he and they reminded me of the inhabitants of a town where Jesus miraculously healed a man. This man was well known in the community because of his dreadful illness. After being healed, he tried his best to integrate with the local community, but the locals didn't want to have anything to do with him, or his miracle. He begged Jesus to take him with him.

'Look, they won't accept me. I can't witness here to what you've done for me. Can I come with you?'

Jesus refused, and sent him back to his local community, not to be a witness to the miracle God had done for him . . . but to their rejection of it.

Perhaps women in clerical collars had to play something of the role which that man played in his local community, now in the wider Church among some of our colleagues who continued to treat us with utter contempt.

Life was getting back to normal now that I'd made friends with the organist again. He and I had fallen out some time ago.

Organists were, and are, rare and vital people in a parish and they often need humouring. Edward was no exception. We were back on speaking terms . . . but only just. Up until a few weeks ago, Edward had been very friendly towards me. After my first service at Basingthorpe Church, this rather distinguished-looking man in his sixties with swept back white hair had marched up to me at the back of church in all his organist's robes and breathlessly introduced himself.

'Hello, I'm Edward. I teach music at the local school, and I've been organist at this church for the last thirty years. I've seen many vicars come and go during that time, but I look forward to working with you as well. Welcome to Basingthorpe.'

As he had walked away, one of the churchwardens had muttered in my ear, 'You want to watch him. We've all had our run-ins with him.'

But over the months, Edward had been both supportive and helpful towards me. We had kept each other informed about music for funerals and weddings, and Sunday services had gone without a hitch. Although I knew that Edward was vehemently against women priests, we respected each other's views and as I was not a priest, it didn't seem to be an issue between us. Edward had also made it clear that he didn't like me to wear high heels in the pulpit. This I continued to do however, and we often joked about them – or at least we did until our 'fall out'.

Our friendship had come adrift over the matter of Education Sunday. The churchwardens informed me that every year on Education Sunday it was the custom in Basingthorpe for the local middle school to come to church for the main Sunday service. The children normally helped to lead the worship and their parents helped to swell the congregation. They asked me if I would organise this service. As I already took assemblies at the middle school twice a month, I didn't think that this would be too difficult a task.

The middle school children had a favourite hymn. It was 'Glory be to God on high', which they sang to the theme tune from *EastEnders*. The whole school sang it with great gusto in assemblies, and so I thought it would be a good idea if we could include it in our worship on Education Sunday. So having obtained a copy of the music from school, I was showing it to Edward at the back of church after the Sunday morning service. He peered down his glasses, first at the music and then at me.

After taking a deep breath he then pontificated, 'Jill . . . this is a song. I am an organist. I do not play songs. I play hymns.'

He had tried to give the music back to me, but I didn't take it off him and continued to further my case.

'I really do want us to sing this, Edward. We shall have a full church. All the children know it, and the parents will recognise the tune. Even the words fit in with the theme of the service.' Then I had tried to humour him by adding 'Anyway, how do you know that God doesn't like songs as well as hymns?'

Unmoved and determined he continued to pontificate. 'He might, but I don't. This music – if I can call it that – is a television theme tune. As I say . . . I am an organist. I do not play songs. I play hymns . . . and I am not – playing – that.'

Holding the music by one corner as if it were contaminated, he had handed the piece of paper back to me. There was no reasoning with him. As far as he was concerned, he was not going to play it and that was that. So I too decided to stand my ground.

'Well in that case, Edward, I shall just have to ask the music teacher at the school to play this song for us on the piano, because I really do want us to sing it.'

Edward glared at me. His face turned a shade of puce. Then with an angry flourish, he tossed back his head, turned on his heels and stormed off up the aisle with his organist's gown in full sail behind him.

We did sing the hymn at the service, but I began to wonder afterwards whether it had all been worth it. Life between Edward and me since that day had been far from easy. Normal courtesies had been exchanged – just about – but our friendly banter had been replaced by stilted and clipped conversations.

But on this particular Sunday night at evensong, without either of us knowing it, things were to change – first for the worse and then for the better.

It had been a typically busy Sunday. I had inherited a chequered pattern of Sunday services in Basingthorpe, and as I was only a temporary figure in this parish, I had been advised to keep things as they were. There was something for everybody at Basingthorpe Church on a Sunday. The day began with an eight o'clock Communion service. This was for those parishioners who liked to speak to God but not to each other. Then there was the ten o'clock Communion service for those who quite liked speaking to God but really loved talking to each other. Matins followed at eleven thirty. I think matins was for those people who didn't like either of the other services, and didn't know how to protest in any other way. There was also the monthly baptism service in the afternoon, and then we had evensong at six thirty. Having preached at three of these services and having had to be present at all of them, I have to say that I was not at my best during evensong.

In Basingthorpe Church, the organ was in the chancel, alongside the pulpit at the front. It was a pipe organ with a high wooden back, and Edward sat to play with his back to the congregation, facing the altar. The pulpit steps were next to the organ. As I walked up these steps, Edward would finish playing the hymn and then swivel round on his organ stool to face the pulpit steps as I preached. This probably allowed him to check on my high heels as well.

It had been a long day, and at the end of my evensong sermon I turned to step down from the pulpit. Unfortunately my heel caught in the bit of threadbare carpet on the top step. Consequently, I missed all three steps, and fell with a clatter out of the pulpit. Edward was at the bottom of the pulpit steps as usual, sitting at the end of his organ stool. Somewhat startled to see me hurtling towards him, he had put his arms out to break my fall, but I fell with such force that I pushed Edward right back on his organ stool and ended up on top of him.

Our respective robes had helped to cushion my fall, but there we were – two people hardly on speaking terms, in each other's arms in the middle of evensong. Once I had checked that my contact lenses were still in place, I opened my eyes to see that Edward's glasses were askew and his hair was all ruffled. I was quite shaken too. But from underneath me he managed to mutter, 'Are you all right?'

'Think so . . . are you?'

'Just about. I told you about those shoes – you wouldn't listen, would you?'

We then set about trying to push ourselves off each other. This was not easy. Organ stools were not meant for lying down on. This one was very narrow, and there was nothing to lever myself up with. I knew that Edward always left the organ switched on during the sermon, so I was desperately trying not to touch the console, and he was trying not to put his feet down on the pedals.

All Edward could do underneath me was to splutter and push. All the congregation could see from the back of church were four feet sticking out at one end of the organ stool. Just as I was wondering whether anybody would still be awake enough in evensong to notice what had happened, I became aware of a person standing by our heads. I looked up to see an elderly woman wearing a woolly hat, holding a cup of water in her hand. She must have walked all the way up from the back of the church. As she silently held out the cup of water towards us, I just wanted to laugh. I didn't know whether I was meant to drink it or whether she had come to throw it over us, because we couldn't get off each other.

Eventually Edward made a last ditch effort to prise me off him. In order to do this he decided that he would let his feet slip onto the pedals to give himself a bit of leverage. This enabled him to help me wriggle back off him. However during this process his feet played about three or four obscure, stray notes on the organ pedals. This was too good an opportunity for me to miss.

As we struggled to disentangle ourselves I managed to catch his eye and inquired, 'Was that a song or a hymn?'

Edward didn't answer, but his flustered face broke into a broad smile. Then his whole body began to shake, and we both started to laugh. No apology was needed from either of us after that. We had reached an understanding on our differences. My fall from grace at evensong had resolved the matter. Life was thankfully back to normal. In fact, this unfortunate experience seemed to have strengthened our friendship. The dozen or so parishioners present that night all wasted no time in spreading the news of our evensong mishap round the parish. As well as being friends again, Edward and I seemed to have managed to become something of a parish item as well. Each of us had acquired a new status and reputation in the community. Whenever we were on duty together we attracted such comments as 'Watch those two. You know what they're like when they get together. We've seen them in action, you know – in church as well.'

The numbers of people at evensong went up too as word spread. As I queued in the local supermarket, Mrs Burke, a regular at evensong, was at the next checkout. We waved across the aisle and afterwards I saw her nudge her friend who then turned round to get a better look at me. As we were packing our bags, Mrs Burke called across and announced to me and all our fellow shoppers, 'Eeh, do you know? I've been going to Basingthorpe Church for fifty years and I've just been telling them all here, love, about last Sunday. You falling out of that pulpit was the most exciting thing that's ever happened at evensong . . . just a pity more folk weren't there to see it. They don't know what they've missed.'

12

Foolish minutes

It was a good job that Edward and I were back on speaking terms again, because not long after there was the most awful tragedy in the parish and a very difficult funeral to arrange. One Friday night, a fourteen-year-old boy, after an argument with his dad, had taken his father's car from the drive of their home. He persuaded his younger brother and another boy to join him and drove off at top speed. Within minutes, the car had wrapped itself round a lamp-post, and the two passengers were killed instantly. Their double funeral was the following week. There was so much anger, sorrow, blame and regret within the families, and the whole community felt their grief.

The young driver of the car, James, was in hospital, but, sadly for him, was not badly hurt. He was racked with remorse and guilt, and wished he were dead. He wanted to attend his brother's funeral, but his parents wouldn't hear of it. James's sister and her friend had been to see James in hospital, and this had caused much anger and distress among other close family members. This only served to make their grief harder to bear. I visited all involved, but my visit to the hospital was heartbreaking. James, the young driver, was frightened, lonely and very distressed. He pleaded with me to try to persuade his parents to allow him to attend his brother's funeral. He felt that only at the funeral could he explain things to his brother and say sorry to him. I promised him that I would do my very best to persuade his parents, and resolved within myself that even if I couldn't do this, then I would find some way of enabling James to make his own goodbyes to his brother.

Grief stirs up so many other emotions and memories within families. It can act as a magnet for every other hurt and disappointment in life. James's mother's grief was expressed in tears, sobs and photograph albums. She was hurt that her husband's grief didn't show itself in the same way. He didn't want all that. He preferred to be on his own with his thoughts. He tended his pigeons and pottered aimlessly in the garden. She thought he didn't care about her or his son, and she blamed him for the argument with James. He couldn't reach her in her grief, and she couldn't reach him in his.

I was often asked in the parish by well-meaning people at times like these, 'What do you say to a person who has lost somebody like that?' It was as if they assumed that clergy had a first-aid box of ready-made answers, which we could take out and apply to people when necessary. Sometimes when they asked, the story of the little boy whose grandmother had just died would come to mind. He wandered into the room and saw his grandfather in the chair crying. His mother tried tactfully to steer her son away, but the little boy was determined to sit on his grandfather's knee. Reluctantly she left him there, but some time later when the little boy skipped back to her, she asked him, 'What did you say to your grandfather?' To which the little boy replied, 'I didn't say anything. I just helped him cry.'

In my experience, much of bereavement ministry is about just that. 'Helping people cry' or helping people to come to terms with their thoughts and emotions after a death is neither an easy nor a passive task. It's one that demands both courage and a measure of involvement. Offering pious platitudes can be a way of avoiding involvement and may be an attempt to minister at a safe distance. Courage is needed too. Sometimes with a bereaved person, it takes courage not to speak. There is always a temptation to fill in tearful silences, and offer easy answers, and to try and make ourselves seem useful. The stark truth is that the sheer overwhelming emptiness and shock of bereavement is not something which anyone else can fill or disguise.

Naturally the church was packed for the funeral service, and we relayed the sound into the church grounds as well. James's parents compromised on the matter of their son attending the funeral. They just didn't want to come into contact with James at the service. I knew that the bodies of both boys were going to be brought into church the night before, so I arranged for James and his social worker to meet me there during the evening. This would allow James some private time with his brother and his friend before the funeral.

I found it immensely difficult to hold back my own tears as I watched James sob and stroke both coffins repeating over and over again the word 'Sorry.' I thought of all the times I, and others I knew, had been young and stupid and done something that we regretted and wished with all our heart that we could put right. Poor James. His few reckless minutes in a car would colour his whole life. After kissing and hugging his brother's coffin, his social worker eventually persuaded him to come and sit with us both on the front pew. In between the sobs, James told us that his younger brother had always looked up to him and wanted to be like him. James then felt in his pocket and pulled out a little tear-stained note that he'd written. He asked me if he could leave it on his brother's coffin, and explained, 'I've no flowers . . . but I've just written this. Can I leave it for him?'

We walked back to the coffins again, and James unfolded the crumpled piece of paper and straightened it out on the coffin. It read

> I know you've always wanted to be like me. Now, I'd give anything to be like you.

James kissed his brother's coffin again, and said another quiet 'Sorry' to his friend and then to his brother. The social worker and I placed a hand each on James's shoulders whilst I said a final prayer and blessing over this tragic little scene. We all then turned and left the church.

It was a tall order, but I hoped and prayed that in time, James' family would be helped to share their grief. Families need to be able to share their joys *and* sorrows. That was my hope and prayer for every couple standing before me during a marriage service too; that they would be given the strength to share their sorrows. Joys are easy to share. There is never a shortage of people wanting to help us share those. But a tragic death, betrayal or a bitter disappointment – these are just some of the sorrows which can divide and isolate people in relationships, and it is divine strength which is needed for sorrows like these.

Jesus had to rely utterly on divine strength. His suffering and agony left him isolated and frightened. There had been no shortage of people to cheer and wave to Jesus on Palm Sunday. His followers clamoured to get near to him. They wanted to be seen with him. A few days later, Good Friday tells a different story. Those very same people who had been so keen to share his popularity decided to turn blind eyes and deaf ears to his suffering, and left Jesus on his own. There was no one with him to share his sorrows – only his joys. Many marriages, when they hit hard times, tell a similar story. Individuals within them all too often discover that the very people who were only too happy to celebrate with them on their 'Palm Sundays' are nowhere to be seen on their 'Good Fridays.' They find out then that in life, Palm Sunday friends are two a penny, but Good Friday friends are like gold.

After the funeral, I felt exhausted. I had been compassionate, dignified, strong, professional and capable throughout all this time, but now I could give way to my own feelings. I travelled back to the church from the cemetery in the hearse. It was three o'clock. Before I picked up the children from school, I needed some time to myself. The church, although empty when I walked in, still seemed to be soaked in the grief of a whole community. I knelt in a pew, put down my books and robes and sobbed my heart out. I cried for everybody in this awful situation whose lives had been changed forever. I was just dabbing my eyes and regaining a bit of composure when I suddenly realised what time it was. I rushed out to collect the children from school. Their laughter and chatter helped me to change gear. Although I often wished that I could just jump into a car and whizz off home with them all after a heavy day, walking home often gave me time to adjust. My own day began to take on a new perspective as I listened in to their latest squabbles, jokes and classroom chatter.

That night I needed to change gear again. It was the Basingthorpe Church council meeting. I had been asked to chair this meeting temporarily in the absence of a vicar. This was a dubious pleasure. The usual arrangement was that the churchwardens and I decided which matters were to go on the agenda, and Ada, as secretary, then typed and distributed it. However, I had discovered that within this arrangement, Ada usually had her own agenda. If Ada considered something to be of the utmost importance to her, then she would make sure that whatever it was went at the top of the agenda as the first item. Tonight was no exception. Item one was in bold capital letters for all to see: THE PURCHASE OF A NEW VACUUM CLEANER.

My heart sank. I frantically scoured the agenda for what was meant to be the main item, namely the bishop's visit to the parish. I spotted some reference to his visit at the bottom of the page under 'Any other business.' He had been well and truly relegated by Ada. The bishop's visit paled into insignificance in relation to Ada's new vacuum cleaner.

Nine of us were on the church council. We met in the church and sat in the chancel between the choir pews. I usually set the chairs out in a circle and in the middle I placed a small table with a cross and candle on it. This was a vain attempt to remind us all why we were there, and what we were about.

I was a little bit later than usual for the meeting, and when I got there Ada informed me that she had already set out all the chairs in a circle. I thanked her and busied myself with some paperwork in the vestry until the others arrived. At half past seven I made my way into church, only to find that it was not just the bishop who had been relegated. The table with the cross and candle had been too. Ada had provided a new focal point for the church council meeting that evening. In the middle of the circle stood . . . the old vacuum cleaner.

We all sat looking at it whilst Ada recounted in graphic detail the occasions when this vacuum cleaner had blown up, scattering dust far and wide. 'I've lost count of how many times I've brought this vacuum up at this meeting and you, Eric, have said that you'll have a look at it.' Eric had been a very tight-fisted church treasurer for years, and had 'mended' this vacuum on many occasions. Ada continued, 'It's clapped out, Eric, and if you want to have another look at it, then you can start being the one who has to push it around. I need a new one. We've had this twenty years to my knowledge, and it wasn't new when we got it. It were no doubt given to us then because somebody else didn't want it.'

Suddenly, everybody had something to say. Members who usually sat quietly and nodded through weightier church issues now sprang to life. Vacuum cleaning experiences were shared and compared and possible makes and models were discussed. Eric was unmoved on the issue. He rolled his eyes and looked at his watch, but this time Ada was not giving in.

'Just tell me this, Eric. How many cars have you had over the last twenty years?'

'I don't see what that's got to do with it.'

'It's got everything to do with it. I can't see you driving round in something that's clapped out and always breaking down. "Equipped for ministry" – isn't that what you were reading about to us all from t'Bible last Sunday? I'm right, aren't I? Wasn't it St Paul or somebody who said it? My needs at this church haven't been equipped for years, and I want to know why that is, 'cos it's about time they were. I need a new vacuum.'

I eventually decided to intervene, reminding the church council how important it was to have a clean church, and how fortunate we were that Ada did her work for nothing. I then urged the church council to come to some decision over this long-standing issue. Eric was being worn down by the women who insisted on telling him about all their mishaps with their vacuum cleaners, and a decision was finally reached. Very reluctantly, Eric agreed to the purchase of a new vacuum cleaner. I breathed an inward sigh of relief and felt a warm glow inside. This could be my legacy to Basingthorpe parish. Some clergy were remembered for great things, such as new buildings, fresh initiatives, and parish events. I might just have to be content with this. In years to come when somebody inquired, 'How long have we had that vacuum now?', someone might say, 'Ooh, we've had it a good few years . . . didn't we get it when Reverend Jill was with us?'

Fame at last. Being instrumental in buying a new vacuum, or falling out of the pulpit – at least I'll be remembered for something!'

My time in Basingthorpe was drawing to a close. It was now six months since Frank had had his stroke. It had left him with hardly any speech and very little movement, and it was extremely unlikely that he would ever return to parish life. A new priest had been appointed, and he was to arrive in the parish in a few weeks' time. It would be something of a wrench having to leave behind the likes of Ada, Eric and Edward, and many other friends I had made, but it had been a good experience.

Not only had I seen how another parish worked, but I had got to know many of my clergy colleagues a lot better. Over the months, there had been a steady stream of priests in and out of the parish on a Sunday. I had stood beside them at the altar and watched as they blessed the bread and the wine. Although their visits had been necessary, they had highlighted the situation surrounding women's ordination to the priesthood. A few priests, who did not agree with the ordination of women as priests or deacons, had offered to come and celebrate Holy Communion, but only on condition that they conducted the whole of the Communion service themselves. Occasionally I had to invite them to do this, because no other priest was available. On occasions such as these, many members of the congregation felt aggrieved that the person who the bishop had asked to take care of their parish, namely me, had to step aside on a Sunday and sit in the congregation, because a visiting priest did not think my ministry was valid. Most of the congregation did, and sadly, this had resulted in a feeling of division between them and the officiating priest.

Then there had been the more supportive priests who were very much in favour of women's ordination to the priesthood. At times even they felt ill at ease during a service where I had preached and led most of the service. They had supported me wonderfully in that role, but they had also found it to be somewhat frustrating to be drafted in on a Sunday morning just to stand up and say the Eucharistic prayer. This arrangement had seemed equally unsatisfactory.

As I began to vacate what had been Frank's study, and my temporary base for the last few months, I came across some books of old church council minutes. I decided to put these in the safe in the vestry. Then, one day whilst I was in church, I found myself browsing through some of these minutes. They were all carefully written in Ada's neat handwriting, and some went back thirty years. I soon discovered to my delight that Ada had never summarised anything but rather she had recorded meticulously the antics of a small group of village churchgoers during this time.

The minutes were an absolute joy to read. She had related the time when the churchwarden had been late for the meeting because he had had the 'runs'. The minutes describe how 'George had set off on time, but was "caught short" and had to turn back.' George's bout of diarrhoea had gone down in Basingthorpe's history. Then, after flicking over a few pages I saw that a special church council meeting had been held to discuss the church fête. This had involved a two-hour detailed discussion covering five pages as to what stalls they were going to have, where the stalls were going to be, and who would be in charge of each stall. Five pages later I discovered the outcome of these long and laboured discussions. Ada's minutes informed me that '. . . we have decided to have the same stalls as usual. They will be in the usual place, and the usual people will be in charge of them.' She had then noted that 'As usual we will be serving scones on the day. Members then spent fifteen minutes deciding whether we should have these scones buttered or unbuttered. We all disagreed on this, but after putting the matter to the vote it was decided to butter them. Members have been assured that this decision will be reviewed next year.'

I bet it was too! I was still giggling at all this when I suddenly noticed that time was pressing. Having booked myself a hair appointment, I discovered that I had only minutes to spare. I had to get there because I really wanted to look and feel my best for my final service on Sunday evening.

The evening arrived. It had been a sad day. The fourth and final service of the day was evensong, and for once at evensong the church was nearly full. As usual, when the time came for me to preach, I walked from the vicar's stall, in front of the organ and into the pulpit whilst the congregation were singing the hymn. I was just about to begin my final sermon when I became aware of somebody on the pulpit steps behind me. I could see the congregation sniggering and nudging each other, and on turning round I could see why. They had all watched George, the churchwarden, follow me up to the pulpit during the hymn carrying a child's safety gate. He was now fastening this gate to the pulpit behind me ensuring that I didn't fall out for a second time! At the end of the service, there was a short presentation for me and words of thanks from various people. Edward remained at his organ and was remarkably quiet during all this. After everybody had finished speaking, he stepped forward to cheers and a further round of applause from the congregation as he and I stood together and waited for silence. Then Edward spoke.

'I just want to endorse all that has already been said, but I will say this. Jill . . . evensong will never be quite the same.' There were loud cheers. 'In fact, as you all know . . . I have seen many vicars come and go in this parish . . . but . . . and I have to say this . . . I have never held one in my arms before.' There were more cheers. 'Thank you.'

I stood at the door afterwards and tearfully shook hands with everybody. Most people were familiar to me, but one elderly lady had brought her friend with her for the first time. This friend was very small, wiry, and talkative. She beamed up at me and held out an eager hand saying, 'Eeh love, do you know, you just remind me of my daughter.'

So I smiled back at her, and, half expecting a compliment, asked politely, 'Do I? Why's that?'

She pulled me towards her, and in front of everybody confidently retorted, 'Well, you see, she's got hair just like yours, and she can't do a thing with it either.'

I was going to miss the people of Basingthorpe.

13

Are we nearly there yet?

It was now four years since I had been made a deaconess, and eighteen months since I became a deacon. There were still few opportunities for women to gain more experience within the Church structures, as women were not able to be fully in charge of parishes. I knew that if I wanted a wider experience, I might have to consider moving to a different diocese. So after months of deliberation at home, and having discussed the matter with Donald and the archdeacon, I applied for a post among the moorland hills of the north of England.

Keith had worked for the Magistrates' Courts' Service for many years, and was looking for a career change into computer management. However, there were the children to consider too. Tom and Rachel were eight and Julie was seven. Without relatives on hand, and no childcare available, it was somewhat optimistic to see how we could even think of moving to a new parish and both work full-time. Donald had been very understanding about my family responsibilities during my time in Deignton. He had allowed me to arrange my days so that I could both take the children to and from school.

The school holidays had been difficult. A friend's daughter had occasionally come to help me out, and Keith had sometimes taken time off when necessary. I had had to catch up on my visiting and other responsibilities during evenings and weekends. It was unlikely that any future employer of Keith's would be quite so amenable, and it would take time to find reliable and willing people in a new place. There were other factors too.

I was not only a professional woman working in a male dominated institution, but I also happened to be a working mother in churches where, in the 1980s, most women in the congregation with children still did not work outside the home. The few women who did work were teachers with school-age children, where day-to-day childcare was less of an issue. Among those who supported and those who were against the idea of women becoming priests, there were still many in the congregations who felt that a mother's place should still be in and around the home. During this period of the Church's history, I was very aware of having to be seen to be professional on two fronts. Not only did I have to be seen to be professional in my work but also utterly professional in my childcare arrangements. Without an utterly professional salary, this was not easy. Although I was paid by the Church as a deaconess and then as a deacon, we had little money to spare as a family and there was hardly any childcare provision available at the time. For this reason, during my time in Deignton I had not felt it appropriate or professional to ask parishioners to help me look after the children. Indeed, there was an underlying assumption in certain church circles that if I and other women were ever to be accepted alongside our male colleagues as priests, then we must be seen to be not only as available as they were, but also as detached from family life as many of them, at times, seemed able to be.

With all this in mind, Keith and I reached a joint decision to take a step in faith. In order for me to take up this new post which I had now been offered, we decided to sell our house and then for a year or so, Keith would be based at home and become a 'house husband.'

My new posting was in the parishes of Helmstead and Burnworth, two sizeable parishes on the outskirts of a large industrial town in the north of England. Having once had two priests and now only having one, there was also a spare vicarage for us to live in.

The vicar of the parishes was Gerald Chapman. My first impression of Gerald was that he was a little bombastic, but I soon discovered that this was only a cover for his shyness. I found him to be extremely kind, wise and firm in his dealings with people, and I could see that I should learn a great deal from him. As well as being vicar of the parishes, he had many other diocesan responsibilities, which took him out of the parish for much of the time. In order to ease his heavy workload, I was to share the pastoral care of the two parishes, and have overall care of one of the parishes, Helmstead.

We put our house on the market and prepared to move into a vicarage. As word went round Deignton that we were leaving, there was much amusement about Keith giving up his well-paid job in order to support me. Our brave step in faith didn't seem to be recognised as such by anybody else. I suppose that that is the case with many a step in faith. We ran the gauntlet of jibes and ridicule from both our families and parishioners. Many thought that we were being foolish, and some parishioners made light of Keith foregoing a good salary in order, as they saw it, to wear a 'pinny' and be tied to the kitchen sink. For them and for us, giving up what was in effect our security whilst working within an institution where the future of women's professional ministry was uncertain, was a radical – and some would say an irresponsible – step. But it felt right for us, and so single-mindedly we pressed ahead.

Our first impression of life in a vicarage was space and lots of it. The children had a bedroom each, and I had a study. What luxury! With no monthly mortgage to pay, as a family we had never been so well off. In addition to all this, I had what all my colleagues had – a 'clergy wife.' Perhaps, with hindsight, I should have heeded the old adage: 'Be careful what you wish for because you might get it.' This role change of ours took some getting used to. It was not easy. I always knew that Keith was both efficient and organised, but the trouble was that I found he was just as good as me at doing so many things in the house. Indeed, with some tasks he was even better. This could be frustratingly annoying. Like many wives and mothers, I longed to be missed and indispensable. I even found myself fleetingly yearning for my old life where men were men, and women struggled to be everything else.

However, Keith was not without his frustrations too. Vicarages were not always well-maintained properties. Old shabby kitchen units and showers that didn't work properly were often the order of the day. Keith found that his days of expertly renewing and fixing were over. He had to wait for Roger Taylor, the diocesan maintenance man, to visit, approve and finance any repairs. This could take forever. After six months of living with old, dilapidated kitchen cupboards where ants took delight in congregating, Keith spoke to Gerald who in turn, after vouching for the quality of Keith's work, struck an unofficial deal with Roger Taylor. Keith was then eventually given a price bracket and dispatched to choose and then fit some new kitchen units for us. He was in his element with this arrangement, and was doubly pleased when Roger Taylor came round to check the standard of his work.

'I have to say, I'm impressed. Haven't you ever thought of doing this for a living? We could put you on our list of contractors then.'

Now that I lived in a vicarage where there was ample room, I no longer had any excuse for not taking my turn in hosting the monthly Clergy Chapter meetings. These always took place over lunchtimes, when about fifteen to twenty clergy arrived on our vicarage doorstep with big plastic boxes full of sandwiches, buns and bags of fruit. I was amazed at how much food some of them were given to eat by their wives. Herbert was one such priest. He was a quiet and determined elderly man, very keen on missionary work. Being retired, he no longer needed to try to impress those in authority. Sometimes this was a joy to glimpse. There was a Christian conference centre in our parish, and occasionally I was on duty there. One day before lunch I was serving behind the bar, when Herbert stormed out of a finance meeting in an adjacent room, marched across to me and demanded a drink. After the first few gulps, I gathered from his grunts that certain people in the meeting would not agree to Herbert's request to increase missionary giving. As Herbert began to calm down, we became aware of a knocking from along the corridor. By now, other clergy were emerging from the same meeting and waiting to order their pre-lunchtime drinks. I excused myself from the assembled throng at the bar, and Herbert and I wandered over to the door of the men's toilets where the knocking was coming from. We could hear a faint, very correct voice from inside.

'Help. Help, please. The door's stuck. I can't get out.'

I looked across at Herbert and mouthed: 'Sounds like the bishop.'

Herbert raised his pint of beer, laughed, and in a loud voice replied, 'Hmmm . . . well, leave him there. Best place for him.'

The people of Helmstead were forthright, stubborn, funny and exceptionally good-hearted. They were quick to argue and pour scorn on others, but equally quick to laugh at themselves. They were slow to agree on anything, and any one of them could start an argument in an empty room. I soon learnt that chairing the church council meeting was an acquired art. This group of people seemed to be quite at home shouting at each other, hurling the odd insult around whilst reminding each other of misdemeanours in years gone by. Villagers have long memories. Frank, the treasurer, was a stickler for correctness in church council procedure. His father had overseen the alterations to the church vestry, which were now causing much concern. Whenever Frank 'dug in his heels' during any discussion, there were always comments such as: 'Eeh Frank, you're no better than your father. He were every bit as bad as you. We wouldn't be in this pickle now if it hadn't been for him.'

My first 'brush' with some of the ladies of the church came soon after I arrived in the parish. One snowy day during the week before Christmas I walked down from the vicarage to the church in order to return some church registers to the safe. Rather than go to the trouble of unlocking the vestry door, I was pleased to see that the main door of the church was open. Some of the ladies were decorating the church for Christmas. Like a lamb to the slaughter I wandered into the church, only to be triumphantly ambushed by Doreen, who was standing by the font at the back of church holding an armful of greenery. She accosted me with the words, 'Have you seen where she's putting that crib?'

She pointed out to me in no uncertain terms a lady on the other side of the church who was bending over the Christmas crib scene with her back to us. In a booming voice Doreen continued, 'I've told her – it doesn't go there. It never has done. It's always gone here by the font. That's where it should go. That's where it's always been. Now she thinks it should go over there. I think it should go over here. What do you think?'

By this time, all the eyes of the flower arrangers dotted around various parts of the church were fixed on me. I stood like a rabbit in the headlights, with my arms full of registers. My next few words were crucial. How I answered Doreen's demand could either make or mar my ministry in Helmstead. I tried to play for time, but Doreen was impatient.

'Well, come on, then. What do you think?'

Inside, I knew exactly what I thought. I wished that I'd gone in through that other door and not bumped into Doreen. Summoning up all my diplomatic skills, I managed to come up with a compromise.

'Well, perhaps if we can't agree as to where to put the crib this year, why don't we put it somewhere it's not been yet? Somewhere it's never been before, and then we'll think about it all again next year.'

Eyes stared blankly at me. I awaited a response. None came. Shoulders were shrugged. Knowing looks and raised eyebrows were exchanged. Nobody said a word. Eventually Doreen drew a deep breath, and with arms folded across her bosom and a scathing expression on her face, nodded first in the direction of her competitor in the crib stakes, then back at me, and then spat out the derisory words, 'Hmm . . . I see you're taking *her* side, are you? I might have known. Typical!'

Poor Jesus – they couldn't even agree where to put him! I suggested that the crib be placed at the side of the altar during the Christmas season. There were general mutterings of disapproval from among the congregation about this, but I was determined to try and look at the situation positively. I congratulated myself afterwards because I did manage to unite the congregation over this issue. Although nobody seemed to approve of placing the Christmas crib by the altar, at least everyone agreed that they didn't like it there, and any agreement on anything in Helmstead was in itself a major achievement and a tiny step forward.

After Christmas we became a divided congregation. We were still one in Christ, I hoped, but there were those amongst us who did not see eye to eye over where we sat in church, and how we kept warm. The big 'divide' arose at the church council meeting when Bert, one of the churchwardens, came up with what at first sight had seemed rather a good idea. It was all to do with the heaters. Helmstead Church was a large, ornate building, and the congregation was a mixture of elderly folk with some young families. Our only form of heating in the church were the infra-red wall-mounted heaters. These were dotted around the church at strategic intervals on the stone pillars. They cost a fortune to run and were totally ineffective. One elderly lady summed up the problem for me after the service one Sunday by saying:

'Well, they're not bad for drying your hair . . . trouble is, when you stand up, you can fry an egg on top of your head, but when you sit down, your feet are like blocks of ice.'

People had arrived at the services with blankets, and some had even given up coming in winter. When a member of the congregation stepped forward to read from the Bible during a service it was cold enough to see their breath. Sometimes Gerald wore his gloves at the altar because the church silver was so icy to touch. Even the organist nursed a hot water bottle. Bearing all this in mind, Bert had suggested to the church council that we should only use the heaters at the front of the church on a Sunday morning, and that instead of scattering ourselves around the building, we should all sit together at the front. This would both save money, and hopefully engender a greater feeling of warmth among the congregation. Some hope! We were in Helmstead. This was a tall order. No matter how often we sang about stepping out in faith, if this meant having to move out of our pew to sit nearer the front and next to somebody else, then for some this was a step too far.

Terse comments were exchanged between Hilda and Bert at the church council, as Hilda insisted, 'I've sat where I sit at the back with my husband – and with his father before him – for over forty years, and I will not be frozen out of my pew.'

Bert retorted in similar vein. 'Well, you'll just have to sit there and freeze then, Hilda, because we'll all be sat at t'front.'

Amidst such exchanges and the usual home truths, we had almost reached something of a consensus, when Hilda put a final spanner in the works by demanding of me, 'And what'll happen, vicar, when we've a baptism and a church full of people? What will you do then?'

After explaining that on such occasions we would just have to use more of the heaters, she rebounded on me with the words, 'Hmm! You mean to tell me that if you come to church like *they* do, once a flood and pay nowt, you can sit where you want and keep warm . . . and them of us who come every week and pay summat, we have to sit where we're told or freeze to death. I'm not moving!'

Although Bert's idea was voted through with a small majority at the church council, and most of us worshipped with a little bit more warmth at the front, there were our fellow frozen rebel Christians at the back to consider too. A great gulf existed between the five of them and the rest of us. Although we all still smiled and waved cheerily to each other across this gulf during worship, I suspected that this was only a cover. There were still pursed lips and snide remarks from some quarters after the service. Whether we would ever really be forgiven by our frozen friends for the great divide, I didn't know. Perhaps the warmer weather would thaw us out and unite us all again. 'Roll on summer!'

Gerald, via the bishop, had asked me if I was willing to consider taking on his part-time chaplaincy at the local hospital. This fairly small cottage hospital was only down the road. Working alongside chaplains from other denominations, I would spend two afternoons a week at the hospital, and take my turn on the Sunday service rota. The hospital service was in the afternoon, so would not clash with my Sunday morning responsibilities, so I decided to say yes.

I was invited by my fellow chaplains to meet them at their customary Tuesday lunchtime prayer meeting at the hospital and then to go for lunch with them all. The prayer meeting was in a side waiting room, just off one of the main corridors. There were about fifteen of us altogether. Amongst the chaplains some were clergy, and some were lay people from various churches who were regular hospital visitors. I just happened to be the only woman. After friendly welcomes and introductions, we bowed our heads in prayer. The prayer was informal and anyone who wanted to speak, spoke. I soon became aware that many of my new colleagues were including a man called Ray in their prayers.

'We pray for our brother Ray who is no longer with us.'

'We thank you for Ray's twenty-nine years of devoted service to this hospital.'

'We remember with fondness our years of fellowship with Ray.'

Eventually we finished our prayers and looked up at each other again across the room, and I ventured to say, 'I'm sorry to hear about Ray. Has he died?'

There was a long silence and people shuffled awkwardly and exchanged glances. It was the Baptist minister who took it upon himself to clarify the situation. After clearing his throat he explained, 'No, no, he hasn't died. It must have sounded like that I suppose. Ray was one of our lay chaplains and it's just that he feels he can't continue with his work at the hospital now that . . . er . . . well, actually, because you've come. Twenty-nine years he's been part and parcel of this hospital, but sadly not any more. You're a woman, you see . . . an ordained woman. Ray doesn't agree with people like you, so he's left.'

I sat there staring at them in a state of disbelief. I felt as if I'd spoilt something for them all, as if I shouldn't have been there, as if this was all my fault. I wished I'd never asked about Ray in the first place. This was by far the most uncomfortable welcome I'd ever had among Christians. Some of these men were obviously embarrassed and apologetic, but I felt I needed to say something.

'I've never met Ray, and he's never met me. How sad that he can't even bring himself to sit in a room once a week with his fellow Christian men and women to pray. What are we about if we can't even do that?'

They all sat in silence. Nobody answered me, but they all looked as if they wished they could.

Life was going to pick up on the following Saturday, however. It had to, because that was the day of the

Mothers' Union trip. The Mothers' Union of Burnworth Church had organised a day trip to a well-known theme park for the children and young people of our two parishes. There was great excitement. Rachel, Tom and Julie had already packed, and it was only Wednesday! They could talk about nothing else.

Burnworth Mothers' Union was a lively bunch. There were about twenty of them and they underpinned the life of the church. Nothing seemed to daunt them. Every Christmas they went carol singing round the houses. One Christmas they plucked up all their courage and went to a home with a difference. A very famous television chef had taken up residence in Burnworth parish. Evidently, he appeared at church once a year at Christmas. There were a few sightings in between – mainly by the organist, Miss Gledhill, who lived in the cottage in the next field. She kept a discreet eye on his whereabouts and reported back on anything interesting when she deemed it necessary. His cookery programme went out on a Tuesday evening, and the Mothers' Union usually met on a Wednesday. His culinary creations from the previous night always provided a ready source of critical comment.

'Did you see him last night? All that fancy food! Who wants to eat all that? I bet he couldn't make a decent meat and potato pie to save his life. Wouldn't know where to start.'

This group of determined ladies decided that they would pay our famous television chef a visit on their carol singing round. Unannounced one wild, wet night just before Christmas, they arrived on his doorstep complete with rain hoods, coats and Wellingtons, and began to sing. They were a bit taken aback when the door was opened by the great man himself . . . wrapped in a towel. Some of his semi-clad friends gathered round him at the door too. He was having a party around his swimming pool. Edna told me the tale.

'Well, we didn't know where to look. Anyway he invites us all in. We stood there dripping wet looking at him, and he stands there dripping wet looking at us. We sang him another carol, and then he says: "Now ladies, how about some sherry and a piece of my delicious cherry cake?" Well . . . we weren't going to turn that down were we, so Joyce pipes up, "Is it home-made?" And he says, "I make everything myself, ladies, as you well know."'

Edna's face then lit up. I could tell that she couldn't wait to impart to me a new, vital piece of information about our famous chef. She continued, 'Anyway not one word of a lie, he goes and brings out this cherry cake and gives us a piece each . . . and guess what? Me and Doris noticed it straight away. Couldn't believe it. All his cherries had sunk to the bottom, just like ours do. Do you know, we feel a lot better now that we know even *he* can't get everything right. We think of him as one of us now. In fact I told him. I says to him, I says, "I've made a few of these myself in my time, and you look as if you've got my problem – you know, with your cherries?" I think he wondered what I were on about, but Doris and me didn't care. We were tickled pink.'

Edna and Doris and the other intrepid ladies were already on the bus when Keith and I and the children joined the queue of people at the bus stop on Saturday for the church trip. But before we had even opened our eyes that morning, we just knew what sort of a day it was going to be. We could hear it. The rain was coming down in stair-rods. When I opened the curtains, the sky was as black as thunder, and the rain was bouncing off the roads. As we clambered aboard the bus with umbrellas, raincoats and bags and found a seat, we were surrounded by cheery comments.

'Oh, it'll brighten up when we get there.' It didn't.

'It can't keep this up all day, can it?' It did and it could.

All day the heavy rain never abated. It dripped off our hoods, noses and fingers. Most of the adults with young children kept taking refuge in the many cafés, whilst the teenagers scattered in all directions. Occasionally, youngsters would prise their parents off their café seats and force them out into the rain to stand and join the queues for rides. Keith and I found ourselves standing in many such queues. With the rain pounding down, no one was interested in making 'small talk.' All the adults stood in a resigned silence, exchanging occasional wet, desperate glances, whilst enthusiastic children, seemingly oblivious to the rain, jumped up and down, eager to try everything they could see. A young boy of about six was standing next to me and could hardly contain his excitement. He tugged at his father's dripping wet coat sleeve.

'Dad, Dad! It's only half past two. We've still got four hours left yet.'

I could see every adult in the queue wince at the thought of the little boy's words. His father, after raising his eyes heavenward, managed to offer his son a weak smile in reply, before tightening his own coat collar against the driving rain. After the ride, parents and children once again retreated to the café where now members of the Mothers' Union had gathered. Young teenagers from our church kept on putting their heads round the door and calling out to us.

'Have you seen this? It's great, this ride. It goes upside down, and you can still eat your chips while you're on it. Are you coming to have a look?'

We offered our half-hearted standard reply. 'We will, in a minute, when it's stopped raining.'

It never did.

Karl was the latest teenager to put his head round the café door.

'Eh, that ride over there . . . that Reign of Terror . . . brilliant that. You ought to have a go.'

We all shuddered and cringed before offering him the usual reply.

'We might do when it stops raining.'

Karl's exasperated voice shouted back at us all. 'Oh, come on, you miserable lot! It'll *always* be raining.'

Edna, who was the leading light and enrolling member of the Mothers' Union, took great exception to this. By now it was four o'clock and even the Mothers' Union were awash with cups of tea. Edna had had enough. She looked across at Karl propping the door open, and decided to make a stand.

'Right, where is it, Karl, this Reign of Terror? Let me have a look at it. Is it up to much?'

Karl was a little taken aback. 'Are you going on it, Mrs Tunnicliffe?'

'Am I going on it? Watch me. Come on, ladies. We'll show him.'

At Edna's command, every member of the Mothers' Union got up from their seats and made for the door. We all gathered our things and trooped out after them. We followed Karl along the paths, past countless other rides and stalls, through the driving rain to what looked like a mini big dipper. On arrival, and without further ado, Edna proudly led her ladies, as if into battle, up the steps of the ride. To sounds of loud cheers from all of us below, they clambered aboard the Reign of Terror. We then watched aghast, as about fifteen members of our Mothers' Union shot off in tiny capsules before our very eyes. They screamed their heads off, whizzing up and down and round and round. The rest of us stood waving and cheering in the pouring rain. Within minutes they zoomed back to us, and we scrambled up the steps to help them down.

Edna looked a bit green and wobbly when I reached her, so I asked her if she was all right.

'Yes, I think so, but I've screamed that much, I've lost my false teeth. They've shot out somewhere.'

Half an hour later in the driving rain, complete with half-eaten toffee apples, cuddly toys, helium balloons, and Edna's false teeth, which we found still in the capsule, we made our way home to Burnworth and Helmstead. It had been an absolute washout of a day, but the rain had never completely dampened our spirits because there were people on that bus who wouldn't let it. The children's enthusiasm and energy had been infectious. It had rubbed off on young and old alike. The children were determined to get as much out of the day as possible, and the whole experience had bound us all together. As our soaking wet clothes dripped and steamed in the heat of the bus, we laughed, chatted and eventually sang our way home.

In and among my thoughts of a hot bubbly bath, and with the rain still beating down on the roof of the bus, I thought about our church congregations, and how much we needed people of all ages with energy and enthusiasm in them to carry us through dark times. God knows there are more than enough rainy days in life. The theme park had been a magical kingdom, and yet, as I looked round our bus, this earthly kingdom had offered me a glimpse of another kingdom. I could see that on our bus, age no longer seemed to matter. Young and old saw each other in a different light. Everybody seemed to know everybody else's name. As we laughed at ourselves and each other, I realised that we were all probably bound together forever through travelling on this same unforgettable journey.

Why didn't we have more parish trips?

14

Doors closing; doors opening

I firmly believe that relationships in many churches would improve if there were as many dances as meetings. At first it came as a bit of a surprise to me how much Helmstead people loved to dance, as they seemed so often to be at odds with each other. It didn't take me long to realise that although these lovely people were quick to take offence, they were equally quick to make amends. I had lost count of the number of times one of our children had come home from church and announced something like: 'Did you hear Mrs Thompson having a go at Mrs Blackwell after church this morning? She was nearly crying was Mrs Blackwell . . . said she wasn't coming any more. Mrs Thompson just stood there and said, "Good."'

Initially, on hearing such snippets, I would make a mental note to see the people concerned during the week. This usually proved to be a fruitless exercise on my part. By the time I saw them, the opposing parties would, more often than not, be the best of friends, and the likes of Mrs Thomson and Mrs Blackwell would each have chosen new opponents with whom to do battle.

Church socials regularly took place in the oak-panelled room of the conference centre, where 'old-time'

dancing was the order of the day. There should be a
decree from on high that every parish should dance, and
dance regularly. Dancing often served to pour much-
needed oil on troubled parish waters. Take Mrs Wright
for instance. She hadn't spoken to me for the last month
or so. My tentative suggestion that we move her flower
arrangement from one windowsill to another because of
the lack of natural light in church had caused her great
offence. However, it was impossible for us not to laugh
at each other now as we tripped over our own feet and
trod on each other's toes during the 'Gay Gordons.'
There was a tacit sense of equality on the dance floor. It
was a place where dignity could be put to one side,
where mistakes could be made unashamedly, and where
wrongs could be righted, or better still, forgotten. The
'Gay Gordons' seemed to have worked its magic on Mrs
Wright and me. As we hobbled back to our seats, our
bruised toes reminded us both that we had a bit more in
common with each other than a vase of church flowers.

Being a woman had its advantages on the dance floor
as well. Gerald, as a man, only got to dance with the
women, whereas as a woman, I was allowed to dance
with both the men and the women. My favourite dance
was the progressive barn dance. I could glean more information from parishioners during this dance than I ever
could over coffee after the Sunday service. There were so
many opportunities for pastoral care in a progressive
barn dance. As we passed from partner to partner, there
was only a limited time to make eye contact and strike up
a conversation. This was ideal when faced with the over-
chatty parishioner. Mr Armitage was one such person.
He thought nothing of holding up a whole queue of people waiting to shake hands with me at the church door
after the Sunday service. Gerald was more adept at deal-
ing with him than me. Mr Armitage would keep a tight

grip on my hand, as he regaled me with tales of his cat, his neighbour and his daughter, whilst people behind him tried to squeeze past us apologetically. Now, on the dance floor, it was all so easy. A few steps together, a snatched conversation, a spin round in each other's arms, and I could pass him onto the next person. My next partner was the exact opposite of Mr Armitage. She was the lady who was always first out of church, never stayed for coffee, and rarely had any conversation. Emily Barnes quite often left during the final hymn so as not to have to speak to anybody at all. Again, here on the dance floor, it was a different story. It's difficult for two people to dance together without saying anything. As she concentrated on the steps and listened to the music, she seemed to unwind. It may have been just a smile or a comment, but the ice had been broken and a contact was made.

During long and tense church meetings when Christians didn't always agree, I often thought that a lot more might be achieved if we could, from time to time, push back the tables, dim the lights, put some music on and do a progressive barn dance.

Sarah was my next partner. She was in her sixties and an excellent dancer. Her husband had been a doctor in the town. Now widowed, Sarah was a shrewd and discreet observer of village life, and had a wonderful sense of humour. She held out her arms for me with a big smile on her face, and we took up our dancing positions. As we were put through our paces, I asked her, 'Was your husband a good dancer, Sarah?'

She threw back her head and laughed. 'I don't know what to say to that. Let me put it this way. He had it all in his head, but it never quite got down to his feet. Dancing with him could be a bit like moving furniture – hard work.'

I laughed too. 'We've all danced with men like that, Sarah. There are a few here tonight.'

The music took us onto our next partners, and Sarah's words about her husband's dancing ability made me chuckle. I have thought about them many a time since. Her words didn't just apply to dancing. They applied to prayers too. Prayer can be a very 'heady' exercise. We can be ever so pious and devout with our words, and then get up off our knees and carry on being the most mean, inconsiderate and unforgiving people. Like Sarah's husband, we too can have prayers in our heads, which never get down to our feet.

I had been invited to a special meal. Our local school in Helmstead was at war. All the children had been learning about life in the Second World War and there was to be a wartime meal in the school. Those of a certain age in our community had been invited into school over the last few weeks to talk about their wartime experiences. I could now see former evacuees, munitions workers, and members of the armed forces sitting among the children round the dining tables in the assembly hall. The hall had been decked out for the occasion in camouflage material, and all the windows had been blacked out. There was wartime music playing, and the whole place was full of laughter and chatter. Every child had a gas mask box strapped to them and was wearing a tin hat. In front of each child on the table was a ration book, which they had made. I squeezed in on a tiny chair between Joyce and Jason and we watched the dinner ladies in forties costume serve us all with spam fritters and rice pudding.

The very young and the very old together are a magical combination, and I listened to them exchange memories, questions and funny stories about ration books and air raids. As we shared food and chatter across the generations, I confided to Joyce that I didn't like rice pudding. She seized on this information, and turned to the youngsters at our table.

'Have you heard that, children? She doesn't like rice pudding. What do we say?'

The whole table looked at me, gasped, and then in a chorus shouted: 'There's a war on. Get it eaten!'

After the rice pudding, the children grabbed their ration books. There had been sweets for sale at the back of the hall during the week, but only those children who had coupons left in their ration books were allowed to buy sweets that day. The meal then finished with a sing-song, but before that I was expected to say a few words. I was too young to remember rationing although it was probably still in force when I was born. So I drew their attention to how only being allowed to have a little of something on ration made us not only value it, but look forward to the day when we should be able to have as much of it as we want. I explained how God gave us rations. Tiny sips of wine and minute pieces of bread helped to keep our faith in Jesus Christ strong.

We ended the day with the famous wartime anthem 'We'll Meet Again'. This is a song of earth and heaven. It is all about looking forward, being back together again and coming home. The children raised the roof with their singing, and in those few moments as all of us, young and old, linked arms and swayed from side to side, our past memories and future hopes seemed bound together for eternity. It was a very moving experience, and as I looked round, I just wondered if this was a tiny glimpse of a heavenly banquet . . . when age won't matter, there'll be plenty of light, and nothing will be on ration!

Working at the conference centre had its more revealing moments. As well as being used by church groups from all over the country for parish weekends, retreats, and selection conferences for ministry, many secular groups used it too. These included craft groups, holiday groups, dance groups and musicians who visited for weekends or weeks. Sometimes on Saturdays there were wedding receptions and formal meals, and during the week there could be funeral teas too. Working days at the conference centre could be long and arduous. There were beds to make up, rooms to clean, tables to lay, meals to serve and washing up to be done.

Some groups were easier than others. A ladies' weekend craft group might not make as many demands on the bar, or be up as late as a large parish group or a big diocesan event. I got used to serving behind the bar on all such occasions and then afterwards joining the rest of the staff in the dining room late at night after the bar had closed. At the end of a long day and with aching feet I would stand around and exchange glances with the other staff across the crowded room. Although willing the guests to go to bed, we always tried our best to appear relaxed and helpful. Often, a room full of clergy would continue to laugh and talk their way into the early hours. Only when the last one had gone to bed could we begin to clear away their buffet, rearrange tables and prepare the room for breakfast.

It was on one such occasion that I was 'propositioned.' The dining room was dimly lit, it was late, and all the curtains were drawn. I found myself standing with my back to an open door, which led to the bar area. I observed a room full of diocesan officials, senior clergy, other clergy and their wives, milling round chatting to each other. Fascinating as this certainly was to watch, it was very late. I was just managing to stifle another yawn when I suddenly felt a pair of hands grip my waist very tightly from behind. Somewhat unnerved, I continued to look straight ahead. A familiar voice bent down and whispered in my ear, 'Shouldn't be too long dear now, and then I think we can sneak off to bed. Are you ready?'

I turned round. It was the archdeacon. Realising his mistake, he leapt away apologetically and was covered in embarrassment.

'I'm so very sorry, Jill. Please forgive me. I thought you were my wife. I really am most terribly sorry.'

It was late, and it had been a long day. I enjoyed his predicament, and we both started to laugh. I spotted his wife across the room, and steered him in the right direction. I noticed that she was wearing a red top. Mine was blue. I pointed this fact out to him and this provided us with a few more moments of laughter. Although his wife was somewhat older than me, we were the same build. I suppose that after a few drinks and from behind in the semi-darkness, she and I were not dissimilar. Some time later, they both passed me on their way upstairs. He and I exchanged knowing glances as we said our good-nights.

Priests, archdeacons and bishops and Christians of all varieties came and went at the conference centre, but I found weekend visits to be particularly interesting. My early morning duties on a Saturday and a Sunday were always the same. Before the guests were up and about, I vacuumed the hall carpet, emptied the ashtrays, cleared away glasses from the night before, and checked the toilets. All this activity took place within a confined area at the bottom of the stairs. During this time, some guests were beginning to wander downstairs for their early morning walk. On a Saturday, dressed in my normal clothes, or wearing a pinafore or an overall, everyone saw me but no one ever gave me the time of day. I was invisible. They all walked straight past me to the main door and went outside.

What a difference it was for me on a Sunday. My first Sunday morning service was at half past nine, and so immediately after supervising breakfast, I had to dash down to church. This tight schedule left me with no time to change my clothes, and so on a Sunday morning I had to carry out all my usual early morning duties wearing a clerical shirt. *What* a difference! As I vacuumed and emptied ashtrays wearing a clerical shirt, I soon become aware that I was no longer invisible to these same Christian people who had walked past me the day before without giving me a second glance. Now, those same black shirts, purple shirts and other very holy looking people, actually smiled, stopped and came across to speak. They tapped me on the shoulder and asked my name, where I lived, and where my church was. Suddenly, because I wore this shirt, I had become a person of worth to them. Some would say, 'I'm so sorry. I did *see* you yesterday when I came down, but I just thought . . . you know. I didn't realise that you were . . . you know . . . ordained . . . one of us.'

I found their difference in attitude towards me on a Sunday both astonishing and revealing. In an overall I was invisible. Only in a clerical shirt was I a person they deemed worth speaking to – a person who mattered. It was a salutary lesson and one that I have never forgotten. I have often thought that many a church dignitary should have some experience in a job which makes him or her invisible and unimportant to others. There are those in the Church who take their authority and the recognition and deference of others which can often accompany that authority, for granted. Whether we wear a mitre or an overall, whether we push a vacuum around or stand up in front of a congregation, we are all people of God, and we matter to him . . . if not always to each other. Jesus drew attention to those who made it their business in life not to notice certain types of people. Unlike Jesus, few of us come face to face with beggars at our gates, or walk past a beaten-up man on the roadside, but there are countless other such people we can choose to ignore in a similar manner today.

I had been in Helmstead and Burnworth for some time when the archdeacon came to see me to tell me that the bishop was to offer me me a parish of my own. I was absolutely thrilled. The parish of Moortown was in our deanery and was ideally placed for us because it meant that our children would be able to stay at the same school. It was a brave move by the bishop in an uncertain time in the Church's history, because women were still not allowed to celebrate Holy Communion in a church. As Holy Communion was always the main Sunday service, the archdeacon was to look into the possibility of arranging for nearby priests to come into the parish on a Sunday morning to assist me. Although our deanery had voted in favour of the ordination of women to the priesthood, I knew that one of the neighbouring parish priests was vehemently against it. He aired his views on the matter regularly in the local newspaper. One of his parishioners often wrote letters to the local press about me too. I didn't know the writer of these letters and he didn't know me, but I regularly opened the letters page to see myself being described as 'this woman in our deanery who is an abomination in the sight of God' and other such colourful phrases. He went on to write 'her ordination as deacon is invalid because her sex is perverse.' In relation to the whole issue of women priests, and me in particular, a local clergyman stated in the press that 'Satan is very active in the Church.'

Gerald advised me to just ignore these articles and letters, and I followed his advice. For the most part I tried not to take the letters personally, but this was not always easy for their content was hurtful. I read them and wondered how a fellow Christian could be so derisory about the call of God in someone else's life. How could this man have such utter self-righteous contempt for me because of my calling and the shape of my humanity?

The archdeacon had spoken to Gerald about the opportunity for me to go to Moortown, and Gerald, knowing the parish and the people, had been very positive about the possibilities for me there. I also knew something of the parish as I was occasionally asked to take evening services there. The archdeacon asked me whether I would like him to proceed, and I said that I would. He was to make inquiries on the bishop's behalf and speak to the churchwardens of Moortown.

I am sure that people sometimes forget that God actually chose to be born in a messy, dirty place. Human lives are messy too, and yet this is where God chooses to be. Christian faith is not meant to be a sterile little package which we carry around in case of need. Faith is tarnished, enhanced, hopefully influenced and at times even governed by life events, emotions, circumstances and relationships. Sometimes in churches I came across people who longed for all this to be different, and tried their best to make it so. They yearned for an ordered, secure, well-defined and unthreatened faith, and often their lives and their church communities were the poorer for it.

I was reminded of this during a beetle drive at Burnworth Church. Some time before, on my first visit to the church, Molly and Peter, the churchwardens, had been giving me some dates for my diary.

'We have a Bible study every other week on a Wednesday, and then there's that deanery meeting we

have to go to on the eighteenth, and then we have a
prayer group. Do you know about that? Well, it's always
on the second Tuesday in the month at seven.'

As I scribbled down all these churchy dates in my
diary, I asked, 'And have we got any social events coming up?'

Molly and Peter exchanged awkward glances and
offered me resigned smiles. It was Molly who took it
upon herself to speak.

'Well, actually, Jill, we don't have social events . . . not
any more. We used to . . . used to have all sorts, you
know garden parties, beetle drives and things like that.
Trouble was that we all kept falling out. We had so many
problems about who did what and when, that all of us
on the church council decided that we'd had enough.
From then on we decided that instead of raising money
at all these social events, those of us who could, would
just give more money. It's much better. There's no fall-
outs any more . . . in fact we all agree on most things. I
think we're a more spiritual church now, and that's how
we like it. I mean, we're Christians. Christians shouldn't
be falling out.'

I'd been new to the parish at the time, and didn't feel
that it was right for me to pass comment at that stage.
Some months later, though, at one of the many Bible
studies, this issue was raised again, and I had said, 'Can
I just ask a question? We're a church family, aren't we?
Does anybody here come from a family that never falls
out – because I don't? In fact I've never even known a
family that never falls out. Just think about it. If you
never fall out, you never make up. And, if you never
make up, you never get to say sorry. And, if you never
say sorry, you never get forgiven. And, if you don't
know what it's like to be forgiven, how do you know
what it feels like when God forgives you?'

I don't think I convinced them, but I like to think that I sowed a seed in some people's minds, because not long afterwards Burnworth Church went on to hold one of their rare social gatherings. It was a beetle drive and supper in the church hall, and what was said by one of Burnworth's oldest parishioners that night might just have made Molly and Peter think differently.

Mrs Harrison was in her eighties and she never darkened the door of the church, although she only lived nearby. The church, and church hall which was part of the church building, were right at the top of a hill. It could be very bleak and wild and it certainly was the night of the beetle drive. Because of the wind, it was also raining horizontally. Dripping, windswept people of all ages squashed into the tiny church hall, and took their places round the small tables dotted about the room. All eyes were fixed on every shake of the dice, as with pencils poised, we were desperate to scribble another part of the beetle's body on our pieces of paper. The end of each game was marked by Hilda bashing a tin tray. That was our cue. On hearing that, we all totted up our scores, picked up our bags and belongings and moved onto the next table, and our new opponents. There was such a buzz in the room. I could hear hoots of laughter, teasing and friendly banter and chatter from every quarter. It was as if someone had opened a window in a stuffy room. To watch churchgoers who had been so intent on keeping their faith safe and secure and untainted, now laugh and talk and unwind in the company of other parishioners was an absolute joy to see.

At the end of the evening Mrs Harrison, without realising it, said something both profound and pertinent. She was quite deaf, and by the time she had put on her heavy coat, woolly hat, raincoat, and rain hood, she was even deafer. Molly, Peter and I stood by the main door saying goodbye to everybody as they stepped out into the night. As Mrs Harrison was leaving she shouted at us, 'You want to put on more things like this you know . . . it's what we need.'

Molly shouted back at her, 'We all give more money to the church now, Mrs Harrison, so we don't need to.'

Quick as a flash and hearing every word, Mrs Harrison shouted back, 'Well, it's not just about what *you* need, love, is it? It's about what *we* need as well. Goodnight.'

Molly and I looked at each other with raised eyebrows. Later on, as we were clearing the tables, she came across.

'You know, I've been thinking about what Mrs Harrison just said. She's got a point. I think we've been doing too much thinking about ourselves, and not enough about other people. I mean . . . what *they* need . . . you know, people who don't come to church . . . Well, that matters too. And if it puts a cat among the pigeons and we fall out from time to time . . . well, it's nothing we can't get over, is it? We always have before.'

It had taken an outsider to move us on a step. Without knowing it, Mrs Harrison's words had reached the parts which countless Bible studies, church meetings and prayer groups had not been able to reach. At last a cosy, safe, secure faith was to risk stepping outside its comfort zone. I was sure that church life would be enriched as they began to discover and respond to the different needs of others, as well as themselves, in the community. Thank God for beetle drives . . . and for Mrs Harrison.

The archdeacon had at last received a response to his inquiries and he asked to see me. On his arrival he informed me that the churchwardens of Moortown wanted, as they put it, a 'proper' vicar, and not a woman. He told me that although fellow clergy would have been quite willing to assist me on a Sunday in the parish, the churchwardens' minds were made up. They had insisted that this was nothing personal, and that they would love me to continue taking their evening services during the time before a new priest was appointed, but they did not want a woman – any woman – as their parish deacon, vicar or anything else. The archdeacon was extremely kind and sensitive, but after he left I was heartbroken. It had seemed like such a good opportunity, but it was now not to be. We lived right on the edge of the diocese, the children were at a crucial stage in their education, and I knew that there would not be another opportunity for me to serve in a parish within reach of the children's present school. Gerald was very cross on my behalf. I was due to take Moortown's evening service the following week. He wrote to remind the churchwardens that the deanery did vote in favour of women priests, and also to inform them that in the circumstances it was no longer appropriate for them to expect me to take their services.

Three months later, I received an invitation to the licensing of Richard Coates who was to become the new vicar of Moortown. It seemed churlish not to go, so I braced myself and pasted on my resigned smile. I decided not to robe with my fellow clergy, but to sit with Keith in the congregation and share our unspoken and private grief of what might have been. We held hands and watched in silence as Richard and his family were officially welcomed, prayed for and assured of the love and support of the whole parish. I was reminded once again of how much being in a pioneering ministry hurt, and what it could cost in terms of exclusion, disappointment and the constant frustration of not having one's ministry readily accepted. The General Synod's vote on women priests was to take place in a few weeks' time. If the vote were to go in favour of the motion, those priests who felt that they could no longer continue working in such a Church would leave, and in so doing, each would receive substantial financial compensation.

If the vote were to go against the women, the sense of disappointment and exclusion which many of the women already had to live with would just have to be accepted and borne. Watching Richard being warmly embraced by both churchwardens, I couldn't help feeling that sitting through this service was probably good practice for that time. If the vote went against us, there would be years ahead of sitting on the sidelines observing events like this. If women were not to be admitted to the priesthood, we should have to bear the Church's decision with fortitude, patience and good humour. We would have no alternative. There would be no money made available to compensate us.

Tension continued to mount as the day of the vote approached. Some of my fellow clergy, like Gerald, had declared themselves over the years to be absolutely in favour of women priests. They had prayed publicly and privately, campaigned, and attended special events and services. Other clergy had sat, almost too comfortably at times, 'on the fence' with the whole issue. This was either because they did not wish to alienate themselves from friends and colleagues who might be of a different persuasion, or because they felt that by not declaring their views they could contribute more fully to the debate, and clarify the arguments for those people in the Church who were as yet unsure on the issue. Then there were those clergy who were vehemently against any notion of women priests. This group provided the local paper with its lead story about one such priest who was threatening to resign if women were admitted to the priesthood, stating 'When I can have a baby, women can be priests.' Another informed the paper that only 'men should shepherd, guard and lead God's people.'

Throughout this time there were regular meetings for the women deacons in the diocese, although some women clergy did object to having these special, separate meetings. A room full of women deacons, many of whom felt excluded and frustrated, who ministered within the current constraints with an uncertain future, gave rise to many symbolic acts in our worship together. These in turn sometimes gave rise to my giggles, which I tried hard to suppress. One such act involved all of us sitting in a circle and wiping the hand of our neighbour with a damp cloth, which was being passed round. This was meant to symbolise and assure us that we were 'called, accepted, upheld and restored.' One of the cleaners just happened to walk through at the wrong moment. Surprisingly, she failed to spot the 'obvious' symbolism, but did however notice the damp cloth and remarked, 'I've never left that, have I? I'll be getting shot.'

Keith and I watched the vote on the television. I should say really that Keith watched it. I closed my eyes and blocked my ears when it came to the crucial time. Then I became aware of someone shaking me and pulling me to my feet and hugging me. We clung to each other and cried and danced around the room. The feeling of surprise, joy and relief was overwhelming. The telephone started to ring and never stopped. People arrived at the vicarage with flowers, food and bottles of wine. With a house full of people late into the evening, the telephone was still ringing. Family and fellow women deacons made contact and we shared our squeals of delight down the phone. Undertakers and

even their drivers arrived on our doorstep. Local coun-
cillors, doctors and parents from school rang me. People
totally unconnected with the church called at the house
to express their delight and good wishes.

Right in the middle of our impromptu celebrations
there was a telephone call from Gerald, which I took in
the study. I expected him to be at the very least equally
delighted, but his voice was solemn and his words
were measured and guarded. His enthusiasm for
women priests had now been watered down almost to
the point of extinction. It was as if he had enjoyed the
struggle and the campaign, but the result and the
future implications were less easy for him to bear. He
seemed to be a different person. Sensitivity for our
opposing colleagues was evidently what mattered now
more than anything else. There was to be absolutely no
place for triumphalism. I should be deeply conscious of
the pain and hurt people like me were causing some of
my brother clergy. Any rejoicing was not to be encouraged, and, if it had to be done, must be done behind
closed doors. I put down the phone and stared at it in
disbelief. I had a house full of people and noisy chatter.
I could hear music, glasses clinking and shrieks of
laughter on the other side of the door. All these people
had come here because they were so thrilled and
pleased, not just for me, but for their church, and the
Church. Should I walk back in and carry on celebrating
with them, or should I go back in and try and turn our
celebrations into some sort of prayer meeting? I had
spent all my days so far as a deaconess and deacon
having to tread carefully and having to be sensitive to
the feelings of some of my fellow clergy. Of course, I
realised that there was a need for sensitivity, but God
knows it was not tonight! I caught sight of myself in the

mirror, and with a concerted effort, I turned away from the phone, picked up my glass from the hall table, opened the door and, wearing a big smile, went back to the party.

Postscript

On 11 November 1992, the Church of England's General Synod passed the necessary legislation to allow women to become priests.

The first such ordinations took place in March 1994. Jill Swallow was ordained priest in Wakefield Cathedral in June of that year.

The latest figures show that there are now some one thousand four hundred ordained women priests working full-time within the Church of England.